Open for Debate

Global Warming

Open for Debate

Global Warming

Kathiann M. Kowalski

YA

BENCHMARK BOOKS

MARSHALL CAVENDISH
NEW YORK

This book is dedicated to my husband,
Michael George Meissner.

Acknowledgments

The author gratefully thanks Katie Mandes, director of communications for the Pew Center on Global Climate Change, for her expert review of the draft manuscript. Grateful thanks are also extended to the following people for their insights and assistance: John Benner, National Renewable Energy Laboratory; Michelle Bisson; Robert Cess, SUNY Stony Brook; John Christy, University of Alabama, Huntsville; Kerry Emmanuel, MIT; Roydon Fraser, University of Waterloo; Jeffrey Kiehl, National Center for Atmospheric Research; Christopher McGinness; Gerald Meehl, National Center for Atmospheric Research; Laura K. Meissner; Susi Moser, Union of Concerned Scientists; Victoria Petryshyn; F. Sherwood Rowland, University of California, Irvine; John Thornton, National Renewable Energy Laboratory.

Benchmark Books
Marshall Cavendish
99 White Plains Road
Tarrytown, NY 10591-9001
www.marshallcavendish.us

Copyright © 2004 by Marshall Cavendish Corporation
Diagrams copyright © 2004 by Marshall Cavendish Corporation

Library of Congress Cataloging-in-Publication Data

Kowalski, Kathiann M., 1955-
Global warming / by Kathiann M. Kowalski.
p. cm. — (Open for debate)
Summary: Defines and discusses global warming, its possible effects on the world, and arguments about whether or not such a phenomenon is really occurring.
Includes bibliographical references and index.

ISBN-13 978-0-7614-1582-4
ISBN 0-7614-1582-3

1. Global warming—Juvenile literature. 2. Global warming—Environmental aspects—Juvenile literature. [1. Global warming.] I. Title. II. Series.

QC981.8.G56K68 2003
363.738'74—dc21
2002155977

Photo research by Linda Sykes Picture Research, Inc., Hilton Head, SC

The Charlotte Observer/AP/Wide World Photos: Cover, 1, 2, 3, 5, 6; NASA/Photo Researchers: 13; AP/Wide World Photos: 29, 40, 81; Corbis: 45, 71; Jim Steinberg/Photo Researchers: 65; Dan McCoy/Rainbow: 96; Coco McCoy/Rainbow: 106.

Printed in China
3 5 6 4 2

Contents

DROUGHT CONDITIONS PARCHED THIS POND FLOOR IN SOUTH CAROLINA DURING THE SUMMER OF 2002. SCIENTISTS FORESEE THAT GLOBAL CLIMATE CHANGE WILL BRING MORE SUMMER DROUGHTS TO SOME PARTS OF THE UNITED STATES, AS WELL AS TO OTHER AREAS AROUND THE WORLD.

How's the Weather?

"Everybody talks about the weather, but nobody does anything about it," wrote journalist Charles Dudley Warner more than one hundred years ago. This book is about the weather—specifically, changes in the weather, and what, if anything, people should or can do about them.

Weird Weather

"Cleveland Sets Heat Record," declared the front page of the *Cleveland Plain Dealer* on April 17, 2002. The previous day's temperature had hit 85° Fahrenheit (29°C). In fact, more than eighty U.S. cities had record high temperatures that week. In New York City, the temperature shot up to 96°F (36°C).

Not everyone was basking in the hot sun. Summerlike thunderstorms, tornadoes, and high winds blew across the Great Plains states.

Less than a week later, winter was back. Cleveland's high temperature on April 22 was just 43°F (6°C). Baseball fans bundled up in winter coats as the Indians beat the Chicago White Sox. Snow fell in Wilmington, New York, as President George W. Bush worked with volunteers on an Earth Day project.

Weird weather continued. Most states had their last frost by early May. During the week of May 18, 2002, however, more than ninety cities reported record low temperatures. Albany, Cleveland, and other cities had their latest snowfalls ever.

Colder temperatures and rain delayed spring planting. Meanwhile, muddy fields cancelled many high school softball games in May.

What happened to spring in 2002? For that matter, what happened to winter? While May was chilly, January was the warmest on record. On January 29, New Yorkers enjoyed a balmy 68°F (20°C).

Some cities experienced an economic windfall because of the warm winter. They spent less on plowing snow and salting roads than usual. "Three Seasons Will Do Just Fine," declared a *New York Times* headline.

Not everyone cheered, though. Ski resorts saw a severe drop-off in business. Maryland Governor Parris Glendening warned about water shortages. New York Mayor Michael Bloomberg likewise worried about a drought. By April, New York had emergency water restrictions in place.

Stronger weather patterns swept around the world too. Nepal, China, and western Europe all suffered devastating floods during 2002. Raging waters wreaked mass destruction and forced people from their homes. For the victims, the heavy rains were more than just weird weather. They were a catastrophe.

But unusual weather is nothing new. The weather generally varies from day to day and week to week. And no year is ever exactly like the one before. Although experience and experts tell us that weather varies, people still feel caught off-guard by unseasonable weather and extremely heavy or sparse rainfall. Despite this, variable weather, in and of itself, does not mean there is a problem.

But the weird weather of 2002 made people wonder. For more than fifteen years, scientists had been warning about global warming and climate change. Experts debated scientific issues, treaty terms, energy policy, and more. Scientists steer away from saying that any single storm or weather event comes from global climate change. Yet now the debate about global climate change seemed more real.

Was the weather of 2002 an anomaly? Or was it a sign of things to come?

The Greenhouse Effect

Global climate change is a "hot" issue today. Are human activities causing an enhanced greenhouse effect? If so, what consequences will that have?

The phrase "greenhouse effect" dates back over 175 years. In 1827, French scientist Jean Baptiste Fourier described how certain gases in Earth's atmosphere absorb energy from the sun. Fourier compared the effect to a greenhouse, but this analogy is not perfect. When sunlight shines into a greenhouse, glass panes trap heat waves inside, and the temperature gets much warmer. With the greenhouse effect, different wavelengths of energy are not physically trapped in the atmosphere. But Fourier got the basic idea right.

Most "greenhouse gases" exist naturally in the atmosphere, but humans also add greenhouse gases to the air. Either way, these gases absorb the sun's energy. Then the gases release that energy more slowly and at a longer wavelength to the surrounding atmosphere and surface. The greenhouse effect naturally keeps Earth's average temperature around 60°F (15°C), warm enough to support millions of life-forms.

If Earth needs the greenhouse effect, what are scientists and politicians arguing about? The issue is not whether there should be any greenhouse effect. The question is how much humans are affecting the climate by increasing the concentrations of greenhouse gases. This is called the anthropogenic, or human-caused, effect on climate.

What are the main greenhouse gases? Water vapor plays the biggest role. It is the gaseous form of water and results naturally as water evaporates from oceans, rivers, and lakes. It forms clouds at different altitudes. It hangs as humidity on sticky days.

In all its forms, water vapor raises Earth's average temperature by more than 54°F (30°C). The total rise in temperature caused by greenhouse gases is about 59°F (33°C). Thus, over 90 percent of the total greenhouse effect comes from water vapor.

Carbon dioxide (CO_2) is in the air naturally too. It makes up about 0.035 percent (or thirty-five hundred-thousandths) of Earth's atmosphere.

Green plants make food by a process called photosynthesis. Using sunlight, the plants convert carbon dioxide and water into sugars and the byproduct, oxygen. Carbon becomes part of plants as they grow. The carbon goes back into the surrounding environment when organisms die and decay. This, in a nutshell, is the carbon cycle.

The suggestion that people could intensify the greenhouse effect dates back to 1896, when Swedish chemist Svante Arrhenius wrote "On the Influence of Carbonic Acid in the Air upon the Temperature of the Ground." Arrhenius argued that more atmospheric carbon dioxide would increase the greenhouse effect. That, in turn, would warm Earth more. Arrhenius said that temperatures near

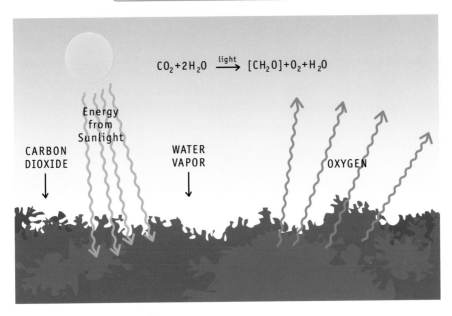

$$CO_2 + 2H_2O \xrightarrow{\text{light}} [CH_2O] + O_2 + H_2O$$

Energy
from
Sunlight

CARBON
DIOXIDE

WATER
VAPOR

OXYGEN

THE PROCESS OF PHOTOSYNTHESIS

the Arctic could rise up to 16°F (9°C) above natural levels if carbon dioxide concentrations increased 2.5 to 3 times.

In the early 1960s, scientists at Mauna Loa, Hawaii, got proof that atmospheric concentrations of carbon dioxide were increasing. They knew that factories and power plants could add carbon dioxide to the air from their smokestacks. But since there were none nearby to blame for the increase, something had to be happening on a larger scale. Scientists started looking more closely at greenhouse gases and their effects.

Since 1750, atmospheric concentrations of carbon dioxide have risen by 31 percent. An international group of scientists says that rate of increase is higher than at any time in the previous 20,000 years. Much of the debate about global climate change focuses on whether and how much countries should cut carbon dioxide emissions.

About three-fourths of the carbon dioxide added to the air comes from burning fossil fuels, such as oil and coal. In the United States, coal-fired power plants are a huge source of emissions. Cars and light trucks play a big role too. The Natural Resources Defense Council says that cars and trucks cause about 40 percent of California's carbon dioxide emissions.

Land-use changes also add lots of carbon dioxide to the air. When forest areas are cleared and burned, carbon from the plants is released into the air and forms carbon dioxide.

Methane (NH_4) is another greenhouse gas. Chemically, methane is the same as natural gas and makes up only about 0.00017 percent of the air. A lot of methane released into the air as rotting garbage breaks down chemically in landfills. Cows also produce methane when they "pass gas." Some escapes from coal seams too. Another source of methane is rice-paddy farming.

Microbes in soil and water naturally produce some amounts of nitrous oxide (N_2O), another greenhouse gas. Fertilizers that contain nitrogen stimulate plant growth, but cause more emissions of nitrous oxide as a byproduct of biochemical processes. Fertilizer-intensive agriculture, like that in the United States, thus increases nitrous oxide levels. Nitrous oxide also comes from burning coal and other fossil fuels. Nitrous oxide can stay in the atmosphere for a century or more before it breaks down into nitrogen and oxygen in the stratosphere.

Chemist Thomas Midgely Jr. invented chlorofluorocarbons (CFCs) in 1928. CFCs were used as refrigerants to cool foods and as propellants to make product sprays shoot farther.

CFCs act as greenhouse gases in the atmosphere's lower layer, the troposphere, which extends up to about 9 miles (15 km) above sea level. Up in the stratosphere, between 9 and 19 miles (15 to 30 km) in altitude, CFCs break down into chlorine, fluorine, carbon, and other chemical components.

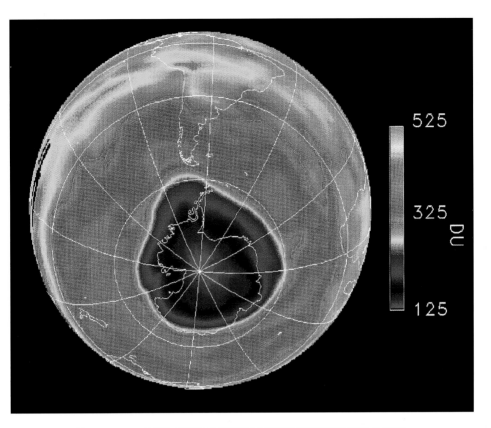

THIS SATELLITE MAP SHOWS A SEVERE DEPLETION IN THE OZONE LAYER ABOVE ANTARCTICA IN 1990. SCIENTISTS BELIEVE THE DEPLETION IS CAUSED BY POLLUTION IN THE ATMOSPHERE FROM CHLOROFLUOROCARBONS.

CFCs also harm Earth's ozone layer, which protects life from dangerous solar radiation. F. Sherwood Rowland and his colleagues at the University of California, Irvine, found that free chlorine atoms bombard ozone molecules and break them apart. This causes the ozone over Antarctica to thin substantially each spring, creating an "ozone hole."

Thanks to an international treaty, the world is ending most CFC use. But CFCs stay aloft for a long time, breaking

America: The Greenhouse Gas Giant

The United States has always seen itself as a world leader. When it comes to greenhouse gases, America is certainly a leader—but not necessarily in a good way. Since 1990 the United States has produced more carbon dioxide emissions than any other country.

Under the United Nations Framework Convention on Climate Change, as of 1990, the United States ranked first in carbon dioxide emissions. At that time, the United States produced nearly 5.5 million tons (5 million metric tons)—over 36 percent of the industrialized world's total emissions.

The United States kept that lead through the start of the twenty-first century. However, in 2006 the United States' carbon dioxide emissions dropped by 1.3 percent while China's rose by 8.7 percent; in 2006, China officially surpassed the United States as the country that emits the highest total amount of carbon dioxide in the world.

The United States also leads the world in energy usage. In 2001, Americans used 2.4 billion tons (2.2 billion metric tons) of oil, about one-fourth of the world's total. The United States is the third largest country in the world by size and population. The country's geography varies dramatically, from frigid tundra in Alaska to hot deserts in the Southwest. Most homes use heating or air conditioning for a large part of the year. Given all of these factors, it is not surprising that the United States is responsible for a significant percentage of greenhouse gas emissions worldwide.

The United States has also had the highest carbon dioxide emissions on a per capita, or per person, basis. According to the World Bank's World Development Report 2000/2001, the United States emitted 20 tons (18 metric tons) of carbon dioxide per person in 2006. Even though China's total emissions surpasses that of the United States, its per capita emissions, which are about 4 tons (2 metric tons), are still far less. (China is home to more than 1.3 billion people, compared with about 302 million in the United States.)

America's energy usage reflects its relatively high standard of living. But many of the world's people live in poverty. They lack not only energy but also basic necessities, such as food, safe drinking water, and adequate sanitation. Compared to the United States, these countries emit minuscule amounts of greenhouse gases, but they may be hit the hardest by any global climate change.

All of this puts the United States in a precarious political position. America emits the largest total quantity of greenhouse gases and has reaped big benefits from doing so. It also has one of the world's highest standards of living. These factors have created some resentment.

Although the United States has not ratified the 1997 Kyoto Protocol, other policy options are still possible. Various scientists and policymakers are calling on the United States to take action to deal with global climate change. Meanwhile, America's position as a greenhouse gas giant puts it in the hot seat in the international arena. The world will be watching what America does about climate change and other environmental issues.

down and causing ozone damage. As more solar energy reaches the troposphere, warming increases on Earth. On the other hand, less ozone would cool upper layers of the atmosphere. Meanwhile, some chemicals used as CFC substitutes also act as greenhouse gases in the atmosphere's lower layers. Their continued use could increase warming.

Other synthetic chemicals play a role too. Some industrial plants give off gases such as hydrofluorocarbons (HFCs), perfluorocarbons (PFCs), and sulfur hexafluoride (SF_6). The U.S. Environmental Protection Agency has called these chemicals "very powerful greenhouse gases."

Soot also absorbs heat, adding to atmospheric warming. Soot is made of tiny suspended dustlike bits of carbon. The black particulates absorb the sun's energy and then radiate it back to the atmosphere. Industries release soot by burning fuels like coal, although most modern equipment drastically cuts the total amount of particulates. People also add soot to the atmosphere when they burn large areas of forest for conversion to farms or building developments. More soot also results when people burn wood or operate barbecues.

What's at Stake?

Average global temperatures have gone up about 1°F (0.6°C) since the late 1800s. Most experts now agree that certain human activities increase the greenhouse effect. Experts disagree strongly, though, on just how much people's activities intensify the greenhouse effect. The Intergovernmental Panel on Climate Change (IPCC) has said that Earth's average surface temperature will increase between 2.5 and 10.4°F (1.4 to 5.8°C) by 2100.

Some experts say that even a little global warming can cause disastrous climate changes around the globe, resulting in more extreme weather. Depending on geographic location and regular climate variability, storms could be more intense. Floods could be more destructive and droughts might last longer.

Global warming could raise sea levels and flood coastal areas.Warmer temperatures would melt some of Earth's polar ice. Warmer seawater would displace cooler water, bringing about a thermal expansion of the oceans.

As with extreme weather events, sea-level rise would not happen uniformly around Earth. Natural geological processes could increase the elevation of some areas, such as the western United States. Areas with decreased elevation, such as the Chesapeake Bay area near Washington, D.C., would see more sea-level rise.

These changes could cause substantial economic damage and human suffering, as well as damage to the environment. In short, the issue is not just about thermometer readings. Rather, experts worry about the effects of widespread global climate change.

Scientists acknowledge that global climate change could bring both costs and benefits to different regions. For example, one area might have increased crop yields from a longer growing season, while another region may become more prone to floods.

Other experts are mostly concerned with potential environmental disasters, such as species extinction, that might result from global warming.

On the International Scene

Global climate change became a topic of international discussion at the First World Climate Conference in February 1979. The meeting in Geneva, Switzerland, focused major attention on future warming by greenhouse gases.

Scientists talked about possible impacts on farming, fishing, forestry, urban planning, and water resources.

Six years later, at Villach, Austria, international representatives began discussing policies to address climate change. Additional scientific conferences during the rest of the 1980s and 1990s repeated the need for international political action.

Political leaders began asking questions. On a hot summer day in 1988, James Hansen of the NASA Goddard Institute for Space Studies was called upon to testify about global warming before a congressional committee in Washington, D.C. Hansen testified that Earth had grown warmer faster than at any time in recorded history.

Later that year, in December 1988, the United Nations set up the Intergovernmental Panel on Climate Change. The panel, which included scientists from around the world, was charged with giving expert advice on the science of climate change. Politicians from the United Nations member countries rely on IPCC data to make policy decisions about global climate change.

The IPCC's First Assessment Report, in 1990, showed that while people were probably influencing Earth's climate, significant uncertainties remained. Since then, more information has come to light. Both the IPCC's 1995 and 2001 reports say there is strong evidence that people are indeed affecting the world's climate. The present majority view is that the effect people have on global climate change is a serious issue that deserves policymakers' attention.

What have the world's countries done in response? One important response is the 1992 United Nations Framework Convention on Climate Change (UNFCCC). To make progress under that treaty, countries have also negotiated the Kyoto Protocol. The Kyoto Protocol calls for cuts in greenhouse gas emissions by certain industrialized countries between 2008 and 2012. The size of the cuts varies by country.

More than one hundred countries have formally approved the 1997 Kyoto Protocol by ratifying or acceding to the treaty. The United States and several other countries have said they will not ratify the agreement. Their leaders feel that the cuts called for by the 1997 treaty are too drastic. Even without acceding to the Kyoto Protocol, these countries can take action to curb greenhouse gas emissions and to deal with climate change.

Organizations such as Greenpeace, the Union of Concerned Scientists, and the Sierra Club say governments and their people must act right away. Among other things, they say, fossil fuel use must drop dramatically, especially in high-consumption countries like the United States. While these actions will be expensive, the costs of not taking action will be much greater.

Not everyone is convinced that governments should act immediately or dramatically. They say too many unknown factors might affect climate. Also, they question whether cutting greenhouse gas emissions would make a difference. Until these and other doubts are disproved, such critics of emissions reductions do not want to take costly actions now. They fear that doing so would unfairly risk economic prosperity. Groups in this camp include the Heritage Foundation, the Cato Institute, and the Science & Environmental Policy Project.

Between these extremes are people who feel that the scientific basis for humans' effect on climate is supported by substantial evidence. While some disagreements remain, they see enough agreement to feel concerned about global climate change. They believe it makes sense to take some reasonable measures now. Groups taking a more moderate approach include the Pew Center on Global Climate Change, the Brookings Institute, and Resources for the Future.

People in all camps think that their beliefs and positions are reasonable. That leaves a big debate going on within the United States and around the world. The debate is: what are the likely causes and effects of global climate change? And just what, if anything, should (or can) we do about the weather?

2
Predicting Weather and Climate Change

How can scientists tell what the weather will be next week or next month? What global climate change do they predict decades or even a century from now?

Weather and Climate

Weather is the state of the atmosphere, or air, around a particular location. It is influenced by temperature, humidity, precipitation, cloudiness, wind, and other factors. Climate is the overall, average weather that an area experiences over time.

Traveling 93 million miles through space to Earth, light from the Sun drives our planet's weather. Some of sunlight's energy is absorbed by Earth's atmosphere and surface. A portion, called the albedo, is reflected back into space. Fresh snow can reflect about 80 to 95 percent of the light that hits it, while dark tropical forests reflect only about 10 to 15 percent. Over time, the amount of incoming solar radiation tends to balance the outgoing reflected energy.

Earth's axis is tilted at a 23-degree angle. The more direct sunlight is when it hits an area, the more concentrated it is, and the more heat the atmosphere and surface can absorb. (Think about shining a flashlight beam directly on a spot, versus angling the beam's light over a bigger area.) Areas in the tropics get direct sunlight year round and stay warm all year. In contrast, areas farther from the Equator get both indirect and direct sunlight. As a result, these zones, known as temperate zones, have seasons of spring, summer, fall, and winter. Even though polar regions have about six months of light and dark each year, the sunlight reaching them is so dispersed that the regions stay cool all year.

As the sun heats the atmosphere, water evaporates and forms clouds at different altitudes. "Clouds reflect sunlight and therefore lead to cooling," notes Robert Cess at the State University of New York at Stony Brook. "But clouds are also a greenhouse constituent and lead to warming." Thus, clouds play a dual role in Earth's energy balance.

When clouds get oversaturated, they release precipitation, such as rain, snow, hail, and sleet. Afterward, the sun's heat causes more water to evaporate from lakes, oceans, rivers, and other sources. The water cycle (also called the hydrological cycle) repeats. More precipitation falls, followed by evaporation.

All areas of the globe do not get equal amounts of rainfall. Landforms, such as mountains, oceans, and land uses, such as cities and large-scale farms, can affect precipitation levels. The Sahara, Gobi, and other deserts get less than one foot (30 cm), while tropical rain forests can get more than 6 feet (2 m) of rain annually.

Wind is another major factor in the weather. Wind is basically moving air. When molecules in warm air move faster than those in cool air, differences in air pressure are created. Air under greater pressure tends to move to areas

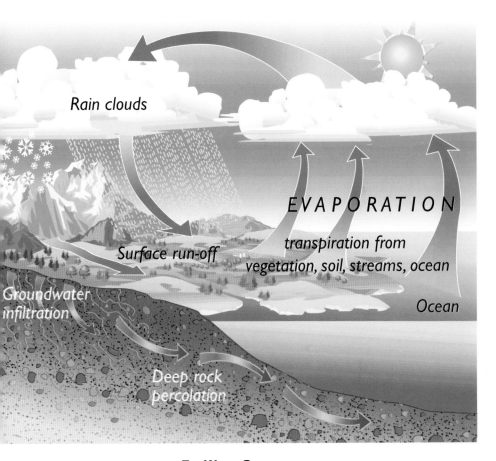

Rain clouds

EVAPORATION

Surface run-off

transpiration from
vegetation, soil, streams, ocean

Groundwater
infiltration

Ocean

Deep rock
percolation

THE WATER CYCLE

that have lower pressure. Air currents also form as warm air rises and cool air sinks.

Some winds are local, while others affect very large areas. For example, "jet streams" between 5 and 6 miles (about 9 km) above the ground may blow at speeds of up to 150 miles per hour (240 kph) or more. Another effect, called the Quasi-Biennial Oscillation, reverses winds' direction at altitudes of about 15 miles (24 km) over tropical regions every 27 months or so.

Earth's rotation affects wind patterns too, in a phenomenon called the Coriolis effect. Earth's spinning deflects moving air and water to the right in the Northern Hemisphere. In the Southern Hemisphere, the spinning deflects moving air and water to the left.

Oceans play a huge role in Earth's weather. Thermohaline circulation occurs when differences in temperature and salt concentration affect the density of seawater. That moves cold water to different layers of the ocean and transports it to different regions. The Atlantic Ocean's Gulf Stream, including the North Atlantic Drift, is one major current caused by thermohaline circulation. It keeps the northeastern United States and western Europe warmer than other areas at the same latitude.

By its nature, weather changes. Air pressure, temperature, humidity, and many other factors bring about local weather changes. In turn, local weather can affect adjoining regions, as when areas of high and low pressure meet and create a storm front. Movement of a storm front can affect even more areas.

Because of all the potential interactions, climate naturally varies. Some summer days are hotter than others. Likewise, some winter days are more mild than usual. One year's spring may be rainier than normal, while another year's autumn may be exceptionally dry. Other climate variations occur over longer periods of time.

El Niño and La Niña

The El Niño Southern Oscillation (ENSO) plays a big role in global climate. Basically, ENSO is a three-to-seven-year cycle of changes in the general circulation of water and air in the Pacific Ocean west of South America. During La Niña episodes of a year or more, trade winds blow steadily toward the west, allowing cooler water to rise from deeper levels and cool the ocean surface off the coast of South America. During El Niño episodes, which can last a year or more, the winds relax and the upwelling of cooler water slows. (El Niño means "the Christ Child" in Spanish. The name reflects the fact that the disruption, when it occurs, often becomes noticeable around Christmas.)

El Niño affects air circulation and pressure above the water, which has complicated and far-ranging effects on the world's weather. Winter storms related to El Niño, for example, can cause heavier precipitation all the way from California to Florida. Farther north, however, the Pacific Northwest and northern states in the Great Plains may have less precipitation than normal. El Niño can fuel floods in some parts of Africa and droughts in others. Likewise, South America's Pacific coast may get torrential rainfall, while its east coast gets droughts. El Niño can also affect weather in Southeast Asia and Australia.

Other cyclical variations in climate cause regional variations too. Shifts in weather patterns every decade or so may relate to natural changes in the Sun's energy output. Other cycles last for centuries or more. During the ninth and tenth centuries, for example, northern Europe's climate gradually warmed. A few hundred years later, Europe experienced the Little Ice Age, which was a period when temperatures were generally cooler. The coldest period lasted from the mid-sixteenth century until the early nineteenth century.

Climate through the Ages

Earth has also experienced major ice ages, called glacial periods, lasting thousands of years. The peak of the last major ice age occurred about 18,000 years ago, when huge ice sheets and glaciers covered Canada and much of the United States. Over time, the glaciers receded, having created the Great Lakes, Long Island, and other geographical features.

In our current period of time, the Holocene, Earth's climate is always moving between glacial and interglacial periods. Today, for example, Canada has a relatively cool climate. When dinosaurs roamed the Earth, however, much of Canada enjoyed a semitropical climate similar to that of modern-day southern Florida.

Interestingly, Earth's average temperature during its major ice ages was only about 5° to 9°F (3° to 5°C) cooler than it is today. Yet that was enough to cause ice sheets to cover large parts of the globe. Just a small change in average temperature can have a dramatic effect on Earth's overall climate.

Recent History

Is Earth getting warmer? Data from the last 140 years indicates that it is. The Intergovernmental Panel on Climate Change says that the global average surface temperature has risen by about 1°F (0.6°C) during the past century.

Beyond this, nighttime daily minimum air temperatures over land have risen by about 0.36°F (0.2°C) per decade from 1950 through 1993. Daytime maximums have also increased but only about half as much. As a result, various mid- and high-latitude areas have longer frost-free seasons than they did sixty years ago.

Indeed, the 1990s was the warmest decade in the past thousand years. The IPCC's historical analysis shows many

Looking Back at the Past

Scientists have been collecting precise data on temperature for only the past 125 years or so. Even during this time span, accurate records do not exist for every part of the globe. How, then, do scientists know what the weather was like hundreds or even thousands of years ago? They rely on indirect measures. For example:

Tree rings. Rings of structures called xylem inside tree trunks transport water from the roots to branches and leaves. Each year's growth forms a separate ring. Generally, wetter years mean better growing seasons, and they yield thicker ring growth than dry years. As a result, scientists can determine when precipitation was heavy.

Ice cores. In glaciers and other large ice masses, the deeper the ice, the older it is. Scientists drill into and remove samples, or cores, from the ice. Conditions of the ice at different depths tell about temperature and other weather conditions from ages past.

Corals. Coral reefs grow slowly over hundreds of years and are sensitive to changes in water temperature and other conditions. Color and growth patterns of a reef reveal clues about past temperature conditions.

Historical records. People were far less meticulous about weather data hundreds of years ago. Nonetheless, historical records describe weather, good or bad harvests, and other information scientists can use to piece together pictures of past climate conditions.

fluctuations for the past 1,000 years. But the largest increasing trend did not start until after the mid-nineteenth century. By then, the Industrial Revolution was well under way in both Europe and the United States.

Natural forces played some role in the temperature increase. But the IPCC found that industrial emissions, land-use changes, and other human activities played significant roles too. Since 1750, atmospheric levels of carbon dioxide have risen by 31 percent. The air today contains more carbon dioxide that it has for the last 420,000 years. And it may be at a greater level than at any other time during the last 20 million years.

Methane too is currently at record-high levels in the atmosphere. Since 1750, the IPCC reported, methane concentrations have increased by 1,060 parts per billion—a 151 percent increase. Concentrations of nitrous oxide and other greenhouse gases have also increased.

The IPCC says the trend will probably continue. Emissions from burning fossil fuels are "virtually certain" to increase atmospheric carbon dioxide concentrations during the twenty-first century. In its studies, the IPCC has estimated that carbon dioxide concentrations will range from 540 to 970 parts per million. That would be 90 to 250 percent more than the 1750 level of 280 parts per million.

With increased emissions of carbon dioxide and other greenhouse gases, the IPCC envisions that twenty-first century Earth will be a warmer world. Though it cannot be sure of the future, the IPCC uses climate models to try to analyze likely global warming changes.

Climate Models

Just what is a climate model?

"That's a term that was coined to describes a set of

CLIMATE RESEARCHER HARTWELL ALLEN AND GRADUATE STUDENT ROBERT HORTON SET UP EQUIPMENT IN A CLIMATE-CONTROLLED GREENHOUSE AT THE UNIVERSITY OF FLORIDA IN GAINESVILLE. THEIR STUDY ANALYZED THE EFFECTS OF RISING CARBON DIOXIDE CONCENTRATIONS ON VARIOUS CROPS.

equations that describe the physics and dynamics of the atmosphere," explains climatologist Gerald Meehl of the National Center for Atmospheric Research. "It's just a big computer program. It's full of equations."

In climate models, winds, temperature, precipitation, and other factors are stated as numeric variables for different grid points on the world map. Equations state the physical relationships among the factors.

Scientists use previously recorded weather information to test different climate models. Based on this information, the computer program calculates what would have happened as time progressed. Scientists then compare the model's results with weather that actually occurred. The closer a model comes to predicting what really happened, the better the model is.

Scientists can manipulate weather in climate models in ways they never could in the real world. For studying change from greenhouse gas emissions, for example, scientists input higher-than-normal or lower-than-normal levels of carbon dioxide emissions to determine what would happen to Earth's climate. If doubling or tripling carbon dioxide emissions in the model leads to typhoons, droughts, or floods, then scientists can understand what the consequences of increased emissions would be in the real world before any catastrophes occur.

Because the physics of weather is complex, climate models are complicated. Computers need a lot of time to make the multiple calculations. Then they repeat the calculations again and again as time moves forward in the model's theoretical world.

"Computer time is the main constraint on what we call resolution," notes Meehl. Even the world's most sophisticated supercomputers have their limits. If scientists are using a model to see what weather conditions will be like in the next week or two, they can use data for locations that are relatively close together. They can take into account local geographic features, such as mountains or lakes. They can better analyze effects of clouds and other climate shapers.

If scientists want to see what could happen decades or even a century from now, they must use data from locations spaced farther apart. Otherwise, the computer could not make the requested calculations within any reasonable time frame. For this reason, many global climate models use data from points 156 miles (250 km) apart.

However, various weather phenomena occur over areas smaller than that scale. For example, clouds affect weather in various ways. But most clouds cover a much smaller area than a grid square on a map measuring 156 miles (250 km) on each side. Severe thunderstorms can occur over smaller areas too. Scientists assign approximate values and estimate the overall effect on the whole grid-square area. As a result, the model's overall global simulation may work well, but it may be less accurate for regional climate analysis.

Climate models do a good job, but they are not perfect. For example, a comparison of seven major climate models found that they did not accurately show all the up-and-down variations, or "wobbles," in temperature over months and years. Yet the models are constantly being improved. They are still the best available tools for forecasting what might happen in the years ahead. Climate models work best when they account for both natural conditions and human factors such as greenhouse gas emissions and land use changes.

"We try to be very clear on the caveats that must accompany models—what the models can do well, and what they have problems doing," notes Meehl. By running models more than once, scientists also gauge how much uncertainty accompanies the results. That lets people gauge how likely it is that a model's results would occur in the real world. "Different audiences want different levels of reassurance or uncertainty measures," Meehl notes.

The IPCC's reports use different terms to describe the levels of confidence associated with potential impacts from global climate change. Those descriptions, based on statistical analysis, help policymakers evaluate the findings and assign priorities for action.

The policymakers' summary from Working Group II of the IPCC, for example, talks about potential climate change impacts. Ranges of "very low confidence" and "low confidence" apply to predictions for which the group has less than a 33 percent estimate of confidence. "Medium confidence" covers the 33 to 67 percent range. "High confidence" predictions would be more than 67 percent likely. "Very high confidence" predictions would be more than 95 percent likely. When scientists are unable to quantify their degree of confidence, they use more qualitative terms, like "well-established" or "speculative."

Looking Ahead

What do climate models forecast for the future? According to the IPCC's 2001 report, average global surface temperatures should rise 2.5 to 10.4°F (1.4 to 5.8°C) from 1990 to 2100. The results come from several climate models using a range of scenarios. Such an increase would be "without precedent" for at least the last 10,000 years, according to the IPCC report.

In general, the IPCC expects land areas to warm more rapidly than ocean areas. High latitudes in the Northern Hemisphere would also see more warming during their winters—maybe 40 percent more than the global average. The National Research Council concurs that mid- and high-latitude regions will be more sensitive to climate change than other areas.

Precipitation patterns will also be likely to change. Northern Hemisphere areas at mid to high latitudes will probably see increased precipitation during the winter months, as will Antarctica.

"The water temperatures in the ocean are warmer, so you have more evaporation," explains Meehl. "And the warmer air can hold more water," resulting in increased precipitation.

Land areas in lower latitudes could see either increases or decreases in precipitation. Summer dry spells seem likely for many mid-latitude areas away from the ocean. Almost all areas would probably experience greater swings from year to year.

With these changes, the IPCC predicts more extreme weather, such as droughts, floods, storms, heat waves, and heavy winds. To appreciate why, one needs to understand something about statistics.

The *arithmetic mean* is the "average" when the sum of all values in a sample is divided by the number of observations. A bowling average is one example. The *standard deviation* is a statistical way of expressing the average amount by which individual observations fall above or below the arithmetic mean.

Many variables, like the height of students, tend to be evenly distributed around their arithmetic mean. The same holds true for temperature readings in any given area. Statisticians say such variables are "normally distributed."

When mathematicians make a graph of the values and the number of times each value is observed, the graphed points for a normal distribution take on a bell shape. In this case, the arithmetic mean is also the mode—the "average" value with the highest number of observations. That makes it the highest point on the graph. In a normal distribution, the arithmetic mean is also equal to the median—the "average" value in the middle of all observed values.

In a normal distribution, about two-thirds of the data fall within one standard deviation of the mean. About 95 percent of the data fall within two standard deviations of the mean. The remaining 5 percent represent the extremes. On a graph, the data make a "bell curve."

Severe weather is most likely to happen when temperature readings are at the extreme high or low end of the range. If global average temperatures were to go up, thermometer readings would be evenly distributed around the new, higher mean. The bell curve of observed data would shift within these higher temperatures. The curve might change shape too and look either steeper or flatter. In any case, the new data are likely to include more cases of what people now see as extreme warm temperatures. That would be likely to trigger more extreme weather events.

Some scientists wonder whether climate change might bring more devastating hurricanes. (A hurricane or tropical cyclone is a storm with heavy rains and high winds that spins around a central area, called the eye.) Factors that affect hurricane formation include winds, ocean circulation, rainfall in Africa, and the El Niño/La Niña swings. Surface water temperature plays a big role too.

"We usually refer to a 'critical' sea surface temperature of 80 degrees [26.5°C] as necessary for tropical cyclone formation," notes climatologist Kerry Emanuel of the Massachusetts Institute of Technology. "When ocean temperature is less than this, the air in contact with the ocean is not sufficiently warm to rise to an appreciable height, and so the storm cannot develop."

If greenhouse gases increase Earth's average temperature enough, ocean surface temperatures will rise too. The warmer the surface of the ocean, the higher the theoretical limit for hurricane intensity. As Emanuel explains:

> **The strength of a hurricane is limited by the speed at which its "fuel"—the evaporation of seawater—can be supplied to it. This increases very rapidly with ocean temperature. In the warmest part of today's tropical oceans, this amounts to 160 mph [in wind speed].**

As a rough rule of thumb, says Emanuel, each additional 1°F (0.6°C) of surface-water temperature increases the theoretical upper limit for hurricane wind speeds about 5 mph (8 kph). A higher theoretical possibility does not mean that a dangerous hurricane will definitely occur. In fact, substantial uncertainty surrounds scientists' ability to forecast hurricanes even without global climate change.

Higher temperatures might also increase rainfall related to El Niño. The IPCC predicts this effect even if global warming does not otherwise change El Niño's frequency or intensity—an issue that is not yet resolved.

Even a small increase in winter precipitation could mean the difference between snow flurries and a blizzard. It could also mean more rain and sleet. Heavier precipitation would lead to more flooding when rains fall and when snows melt in the spring.

Droughts would be more frequent in a warmer world too, according to climate models. At first glance, the forecast seems inconsistent with warnings of wetter weather. But both are a concern, depending on the time of year, says climatologist Meehl. There might be more rainfall during the winter, but less during the summer, when drought is usually a problem.

Also, rainfall is often unevenly distributed. Much of India suffered from drought during the summer of 2002, for example. In some parts of India and south Asia, however, floods forced thousands of people to flee their homes.

Sea-level rise would also be a consequence of a warmer world since warmer ocean water expands to take up more space. A warmer climate would also speed the melting of glaciers and ice caps. The less ice cover there is to reflect sunlight back into space, the more heat can be absorbed by darker oceans and land. That raises temperatures more and compounds the effects of warming.

Just as an ice cube melting in a half full glass of water does not make the water overflow, ice floes melting into the ocean will not raise sea levels. However, ice melting

Is the Ice Already Melting?

At more than 17,000 feet (5,182 m) above sea level, Bolivia's Chacaltaya Mountain hosts the world's highest ski slope. Within fifteen years, however, the mountain's glacier may melt. The Byrd Polar Research Center at Ohio State University says that within the last thirty years, the Andean glaciers have shrunk by up to 25 percent. The news alarms not only skiers, but also the 1.5 million people in and near La Paz who rely on the glaciers for their water.

Glaciers are also shrinking atop the massive Himalayas north of India. If the present melting rate continues, says the environmental activist group Greenpeace, those glaciers might be gone by 2035. That would jeopardize the drinking water source for up to a billion people.

Other cold spots are warming up too. Reporting from Svalbard, Norway, scientists aboard the Greenpeace flagship *Rainbow Warrior* said that glaciers on Arctic islands were retreating up to 492 feet (150 m) per year. "If global warming continues as the climate models predict, we can expect an accelerated retreat of these glaciers in the future," said University of Oslo professor Ove Hagen.

In another study, University of Alaska researchers measured the thickness of various Alaskan glaciers. On average, from the 1950s to the 1990s, the glaciers lost just over half a yard (half a meter) of thickness per year. From the mid-1990s until 2001, however, the glaciers lost an average of 6 feet (1.8 m) of thickness per year. The findings suggest that sea-level rise could be even greater than the IPCC anticipates. For groups concerned about climate change, that news is chilling.

In 2002, an area of Antarctica's Larsen B Ice Shelf as big as Rhode Island broke off. With an estimated age of 9,000 to 12,000 years, the shelf had already been floating on water. Thus, its collapse did not raise sea levels. But scientists like Eugene Domack at Hamilton College in New York think the warming that led to the disintegration of the ice shelf was "extraordinary." Oceans surrounding Antarctica are warming, and the Antarctic summer that started in December 2001 was unusually warm.

Curiously, other parts of Antarctica showed less warming, or even slight cooling trends. Areas near the South Pole have added snow and ice in recent decades, report researchers from Ohio State University. Some parts of Greenland also seem to be accumulating ice.

Like other phenomena, the growth or shrinkage of ice sheets is not uniform around the globe. In part, this suggests a need for more study. As a practical matter, it underscores the idea that global climate change will have varied effects around the world.

over the landmasses of Antarctica, Alaska, and Greenland, could speed the breakup of glaciers into large masses, which would then slide into the sea. That would be like plopping ice cubes into an already full glass.

By 2100, the IPCC expects average sea levels around the globe to increase between 4 and 34 inches (10 and 88 cm) over 1990 levels. The amount of increase will vary from region to region around the globe.

What does all of this mean? Presently, most scientists feel some concern about global climate change. Extreme weather such as storms, floods, and droughts already causes serious problems around the world. Increases in those climate-related impacts could mean significantly more losses of life, land, and property. Thus, climate change and its impacts deserve ongoing study and investigation. Many also feel that it makes sense to reduce greenhouse gas emissions and to develop ways to deal with the most likely and serious climate-change impacts.

The Worst-Case Scenarios

Some environmental activists fear that global climate change will cause countless disasters unless people take drastic steps now. While other scientists and policymakers are not as alarmist about the problem, they feel the scientific evidence shows that some global climate change will occur. Thus, they ask the question, "What's the worst that could happen?" Based on the answers, it may make sense to take some actions now to prevent or control the most serious and likely consequences.

Stormy Weather

Floyd was fierce. Wind speeds for the 1999 hurricane reached 155 mph (250 kph) at the eye wall. Even at the storm's weaker edge, winds whipped at up to 73 mph (117 kph).

Hurricane Floyd forced large numbers of people to evacuate their homes in the southeastern United States. It destroyed or damaged over 67,000 homes. Twelve thousand

awareness about the impacts of extreme weather. Both voters and policymakers become more inclined to listen to concerns about the potential impacts of climate change.

Scientists cannot say if warming from greenhouse gases will make future El Niños worse. Because ENSO cycles last several years, researchers do not yet have enough data. Yet even the possibility is scary. In February 1998, for example, El Niño–related storms swept across California. Coastal areas were awash in up to 6 feet (1.8 m) of rain. Mudslides destroyed million-dollar homes. With crops also destroyed, many poor farm laborers found themselves out of work. Who wants anything worse?

Drying Up

More than half of the United States went through a drought during 2002. Farmers worried about their crops. Cities like Greensboro, North Carolina, and Denver, Colorado, placed limits on watering lawns and gardens and washing cars. People who broke the law risked paying fines or having their water shut off.

Meanwhile, many western states fought brush and forest fires. By mid-June, one fire had destroyed more than 100,000 acres of Pike National Forest in Colorado. By early August, about 300,000 acres were ablaze in Oregon's giant Florence fire. Climate models have shown that such droughts and their accompanying disasters will happen more often in a warmer world.

Droughts can spell disaster for farmers, though they can adapt to occasional dry seasons by planting different crops. In India, for example, farmers may prefer to plant groundnuts and soybeans in wet years. Generally, both protein-rich crops bring good prices. Farmers can plant millet, though, if they know the growing season will not be wet enough for the other crops. But farmers do not always have those choices, and forecasts are not always accurate. Thus, droughts can still cost farmers their harvests—and their livelihoods.

In a warming world, places like Africa and Asia would likely be hardest hit by droughts. Many of their farmers lack modern irrigation and other technologies that industrialized countries rely on.

The United Nations Environment Programme (UNEP) has said that each additional degree Celsius of average temperature could cut grain production in the tropics by up to 10 percent. Cash crops like coffee and tea would suffer too, crippling some countries' economies. Klaus Toepfer of the UNEP warned:

Billions of people across the tropics depend on crops such as rice, maize and wheat for their very survival. . . . [L]arge numbers are facing acute hunger and malnutrition unless the world acts to reduce emissions of carbon dioxide and other greenhouse gases.

"About a billion people still don't have adequate drinking water," adds Susi Moser of the Union of Concerned Scientists. Droughts mean even less water. Floods would not help either. Their uncontrolled overflow destroys villages and creates serious sanitation problems. "We're already vulnerable," warns Moser. "Then you change something like that, and we're going to be in severe conflict over these limited resources."

As in the present, future food and water shortages would hurt poor people the most. After all, in a free-market economy, laws of supply and demand apply. Richer people can afford to pay the higher prices caused by shortages, while poorer people are shut out of the market. Millions of poor people already go to bed each night suffering from hunger and malnutrition. A warmer world might increase that misery.

Dusty Disaster

In the Great Plains states, the Great Depression of the 1930s was sparked by years of prolonged drought following the stock market crash. Without enough rain to grow their crops, farmers across this area faced financial ruin.

Vast prairies covered most of the Great Plains before the many farmers and ranchers settled there. During droughts, the grasses might go dormant, but their roots would still cling to the soil. During the early twentieth century, however, farmers had plowed millions of acres. With no roots holding it in place, dry topsoil could be easily blown away.

Winds swept across the prairies and blanketed everything with fine, sooty dust. Bad windstorms produced "black blizzards"—dust storms so thick that they blacked out sunlight. Even on days without storms, dirt covered beds, tables, and even cupboard shelves. Dust was literally everywhere during the Dust Bowl years.

Dust and dirt were not the only problems. Bad harvests left farm families with no money. Banks foreclosed on mortgages. Before long, half of Oklahoma's population needed public assistance, or welfare, to survive.

Things got so bad that hundreds of thousands of "Okies" left their homes in Oklahoma and other Great Plains states. They went west to California, hoping for a better life. Yet California could offer few good jobs during the Depression. Instead, many people became migrant workers and toiled in the sun for meager wages.

Modern conservation techniques reduce soil erosion. But droughts can still spell disaster, as could a sudden climate change.

DUST STORMS LIKE THIS ONE RAVAGED OKLAHOMA AND OTHER GREAT PLAINS STATES DURING THE 1930S. THE DUST BOWL IS AN EXAMPLE OF HOW DRAMATIC ECOLOGICAL AND ECONOMIC CONSEQUENCES CAN RESULT FROM CHANGES IN NORMAL PRECIPITATION PATTERNS.

Health Hazards

More than 500 people died from heat-related causes when a heat wave struck Chicago in July 1995. The 2003 heat wave in Europe had an even higher death toll. Thirty-five thousand deaths resulted from the weeks of unusually high temperatures across the continent. During the hot summer days of 2006, hundreds of men and women died in California. Each year, it seems, record temperatures—over 112° in Arizona for ten straight days in 2007—cause more health problems for more people. Climate change could bring more killer heat waves.

Poor people and the elderly are most vulnerable to heat's health problems. They are less likely to have air conditioning and they may not have money or ready access to good health care.

Higher temperatures could also spur overgrowth of ragweed and other plants that could cause trouble for allergy sufferers. Hot weather also increases the smog problem in cities. Poor air quality irritates the lungs of people with asthma and other respiratory diseases. In short, fewer people would breathe easily in a warmer world.

Global climate change can cause other health problems too. As storms and floods destroy homes and businesses, they ruin clean water and food supplies, as well as drainage and wastewater-treatment systems. After Hurricane Mitch struck Central America in 1998, for example, thousands of people got cholera from drinking contaminated water. Besides vomiting and severe diarrhea, the disease causes dehydration, shock, and can cause death.

Even in the United States, about half the waterborne-disease outbreaks during the last fifty years have happened after heavy rainfalls. Acute gastrointestinal illness was the most common disease; symptoms include severe vomiting, cramps, and diarrhea. "The significance of the association between precipitation and disease is amplified when you consider the effects of global climate change, which predict an increase in precipitation in parts of the United States," said Jonathan Patz of the Johns Hopkins Bloomberg School of Public Health.

Severe storms destroy homes too. By necessity, displaced people are often forced to live more closely together. That, in turn, increases the risk of tuberculosis and other airborne diseases.

Even without severe storms, warmer, wetter weather could mean more sickness. Mosquitoes, ticks, sand flies, and other pests act as disease vectors. In other words, they carry and transmit bacteria, viruses, and other infectious agents.

Warmer weather could increase the geographic range for insects like mosquitoes. Higher temperatures might increase the insects' metabolism too. That could make them breed and bite more actively.

Malaria, a mosquito-spread disease, causes cycles of fever, sweats, and chills. It kills between 1 and 3 million people each year. Paul Epstein of the Harvard School of Public Health and Jonathan Patz of Johns Hopkins University suggest that climate change could increase the range in the tropics and subtropics where malaria is most widespread. Additionally, climate change could enable infected mosquitoes to thrive more readily at higher altitudes in Africa and elsewhere. According to the World Health Organization, malaria has already spread to the Colombian Andes, which are 7,000 feet (2,134 m) above sea level. The result could be up to a million more malaria deaths per year by the middle of the twenty-first century.

Malaria is not the only potential menace from mosquitoes. Dengue fever is a flulike viral infection that causes fever, headache, hideous bone pain, and backache. Yellow fever causes similar symptoms, as well as bleeding gums, bloody urine, and jaundice (a liver problem that causes a yellowish complexion). Rift Valley fever is a viral disease that produces acute fever, shock, vision loss, brain problems, and hemorrhages (bleeding). All these diseases might become more widespread with global climate change.

Encephalitis is a disease that infects the brain. Mosquitoes, ticks, and other insects transmit the disease. In one study, researchers linked warmer weather to outbreaks of tick-transmitted encephalitis in Sweden.

West Nile virus is a type of encephalitis that usually occurs in Africa, western Asia, and the Middle East. Since 1999, West Nile virus has invaded the United States. More than 4,260 people got the disease in 2006, and about 177 people died of it.

The Centers for Disease Control and Prevention (CDC) has linked West Nile virus to at least one mosquito species that can overwinter, or survive the winter in temperate climates. Droughts may play a role in the spread of this virus too. Sometimes, less water means fewer breeding grounds, and thus fewer mosquitoes. Other times, droughts can increase the number of small, stagnant puddles where mosquitoes can breed or cut down the numbers of insects and amphibians that prey on mosquitoes. Global climate change could bring even more outbreaks of West Nile virus.

Hantavirus is another hazard. No one in modern America had suffered from the disease until 1993. Then a mysterious outbreak occurred in the Four Corners area of the southwestern United States (a large region around the intersection of Arizona, New Mexico, Colorado, and Utah). Racing against the clock, medical personnel from the CDC, state agencies, and other groups finally identified the disease and were able to control it.

Scientists linked the hantavirus outbreak to higher-than-usual populations of deer mice after a very moist winter because of El Niño. This wetter weather made it possible for more mice to breed and thrive, causing more competition for food in the desert. As a result, the mice ventured closer to populated areas than they normally would have. That brought people into closer contact with the mice droppings and urine, which carry the contagious virus. Since, according to the IPCC, climate change can cause heavier winter precipitation, hantavirus could become a greater public health problem.

Black flies spread onchocerciasis, or "river blindness." Presently, the disease occurs mostly in West Africa and Latin America. Under some climate models, West Africa's black fly populations could increase by 25 percent, possibly causing more cases of the disease. Likewise, increased populations of tsetse flies would mean more cases of African trypanosomiasis, or "sleeping sickness." The symptoms of that potentially fatal disease include extreme fatigue.

Uncertainty naturally accompanies all of these predictions. Making matters more complicated is that epidemiology, the study of the spread of disease, is itself an intricate subject. Economics and lifestyle matter a lot too. Poor people in less-developed nations have long had higher risks of deadly diseases. People in industrialized countries by and large have better health care and can better adapt to higher risks.

From 1980 to 1999, for example, dengue fever was a much bigger problem in Mexico than in nearby Texas. Texas had only 64 cases, while three Mexican border states had more than 62,000 cases. A stronger economy and higher standard of living make access to air conditioning, pesticides, and window screens more common in the United States. America's public health system tends to be much better too.

It is clear that many factors besides climate play a role in the spread and control of disease. Despite this, some public health experts worry that global climate change may make a bad problem like infectious disease even worse.

Rising Waters

By 2100, the IPCC expects average sea levels to rise between 4 and 34 inches (10 and 88 cm) over 1990 levels. The amount of increase will not be the same all around the globe, but will vary from region to region.

"You can never excite anybody with a foot or two of sea-level rise over a long time period," admits Moser. "The issue with sea-level rise is that it will make coastal storms, coastal flooding, and coastal erosion—things that are already severe problems—so much worse."

About half of the world's people live within 38 miles (60 km) of the coast. A sea-level rise of 20 inches (50 cm) could expose more than 90 million people to annual flooding. That is about twice the number who presently live with that risk, according to an estimate reported in the *British Medical Journal*.

In Bangladesh, for example, about 6 million people presently live in low-lying areas that are less than 3 feet (almost 1 m) above sea level. If sea level were to rise just a foot (30 cm), many would lose their homes and their livelihoods. Likewise, in southern and eastern Asia, sea-level rise might cut rice production up to 10 percent.

Elsewhere, beautiful beaches could soon be below water. Geology professor Mark Meier at the University of Colorado has suggested that just one foot (30 cm) of sea-level rise could push shorelines back 100 feet (30 meters). That could spell economic ruin for the Bahamas, Jamaica, and other beach areas that rely on tourist dollars.

Even the United States could be at risk. About half of its almost 280 million people live within 50 miles (80 km) of the shore. Within fifty years, sea level around New York could go up by 20 inches (50 cm). By 2080, storms could flood Manhattan's financial district and tunnels. Farther south along the east coast, higher sea levels could harm wildlife habitats.

Sea-level rise could threaten fresh drinking water supplies too. Many people use groundwater that they pump from underground sources. In coastal areas, changes in sea level can cause saltwater incursion into freshwater aquifers, making the freshwater undrinkable. If annual rainfall decreased, the amount of freshwater could shrink even more.

Wreaking Havoc with Habitats

"Imagine Baltimore *without* the Baltimore oriole," said National Wildlife Federation president Mark Van Putten. A study by the group said that global climate change could displace the range of Maryland's state bird. Range shifts could also affect many other birds, such as the California quail, the American goldfinch, the purple finch, the black-capped chickadee, and the brown thrush.

Scientists already see signs that global climate change is affecting plants and animals. Researchers in Great Britain found that the first-flowering date for nearly 400 plant species there had moved up an average of 4.5 days during the 1990s. Over time, such changes could affect competition, potential breeding, and other interactions among species.

A different study suggested that global climate change is already altering hatching times for insects like the winter moth. If the caterpillars hatch before oak leaves are on the trees, they do not have enough food to eat. The moths' decline can have ripple effects along the food chain. Insect-eating birds will have less food. Weasels and hawks that prey on the birds will likewise find less to eat.

As weather patterns change, so may wildlife habitat patterns. In a warmer world, some species may move northward or uphill while others may shrink into smaller habitat areas. The reshuffling will bring new species of predators and prey together. Different groups of species will compete for resources.

Fish may also feel the heat of global warming. Within

fifty years, the boundary between warm-water and cold-water fish species may shift northward by 300 miles (480 km). Some species may fare better in a warmer world. Others, like trout, whitefish, salmon, and walleye, could find themselves displaced. Climate change may directly affect the numbers of certain fishes, such as salmon.

Coral reefs are also at risk. They build up over time from the shells of tiny invertebrate animals. Healthy coral reefs harbor many types of marine plant and animal life. They also provide protection for the coast, significant tourist income, scenic beauty, and a source of ingredients for new drugs. Some of the world's most beautiful coral reefs lie off the coasts of Australia, Florida, and the Caribbean Islands.

Coral reef systems thrive only in a narrow temperature margin. Colorful microscopic organisms called zooanthellae usually live among the coral and provide food for other organisms. If the water gets too warm, stressed coral expel the zooanthellae, turn white or "bleach," and sometimes die. Over time, extensive bleaching damages whole reefs. A Greenpeace report found that global climate change could make severe coral bleaching an annual event in less than three decades.

"The world's coral reefs are sending out an S.O.S.," noted Greenpeace's climate policy specialist Iain MacGill. "The loss of coral reefs would have devastating consequences, adversely affecting millions of people around the world."

Even if rising seas did not wash them away, more than a dozen Pacific island nations would face near-total social and economic disaster, claims Greenpeace. Fisheries that depend on coral reefs for food and shelter would suffer, leaving a dwindling food supply for the islands' growing populations. The islands would have less coastal protection and more land erosion. Tourist dollars would dry up too.

Climate change likewise threatens coastal wetlands.

Wetlands are valuable ecological resources that filter pollutants out of soil and water. Sea-level rise could squeeze out wetlands and the species that live there.

"Wetlands would naturally migrate inland," notes Moser. They would re-establish themselves based on the new shoreline. "But if you build roads there, if you have bulkheads and seawalls and all these obstacles that they can't get over, they get squeezed out and eventually get lost," she says. "What would that mean? You lose your fisheries that depend on them."

Global climate change could also ruin alpine habitats. Mountain species thrive on cooler temperatures at higher altitudes. Global climate change could make those areas too warm for the plants and animals that live there.

"They will adapt by going higher and higher up on the mountain to continue to live in the temperature range that they like," notes Moser. "Well, eventually, they'll fall off the top of the mountain, because there's no other place to go. They're going to be gone."

Large areas of rain forest are at risk and could die as temperature or water conditions change. This would be disastrous because about half of the world's species live in rain forests and many of them would die along with the forests. Already, the Sierra Club has linked declines of frog and lizard species in Costa Rica's Monteverde Cloud Forest to warmer Pacific Ocean temperatures.

In other areas, drying grasslands could change into deserts. Desertification is currently a problem in parts of Africa.

Climate change could hurt species in cooler climates too. New England's brilliant fall foliage could fade into history. Unless winters stay cold enough, the maple syrup industry could dry up. Besides messing with the ecosystem, climate change could hurt the skiing industry and tourism.

Climate change could cause havoc even in the higher latitudes. Antarctic krill eat algae that grow under sea ice. As sea ice shrinks, krill populations could decline, leaving penguins, albatrosses, seals, and other krill predators with less food.

Alaska may already be showing effects of climate change. As of 2002, over 90 percent of the spruce trees on Alaska's Kenai Peninsula lay dead or dying, victims of an unusually large beetle infestation. Botanist Edward Berg at the Kenai National Wildlife Refuge determined that several years of warmer summers doubled the reproduction rate for spruce bark beetles.

While people might adapt to quick climate changes, forests that take thousands of years to grow cannot. Indeed, plants' predicted rates of evolution generally lag behind anticipated rates of climate change. A 2006 article in *Time* magazine reported that more than one million species of plants and animals could become extinct by 2050. Once fragile habitats are destroyed, they may never recover. Once a species is extinct, it literally has no tomorrow.

Economic and Political Turmoil

More extreme weather, higher rates of disease, and ecological harm all bring heavy costs to the planet, but developing nations and their people will probably bear the biggest burdens. Geographic location makes these countries very vulnerable to extreme weather. Also, because many of these countries have poor infrastructures, they lack decent health care, adequate sanitation, safe drinking-water supplies, and good transportation networks. When disaster strikes, what little they have may get wiped out. In other words, developing countries often lack options for a quick response and recovery.

To make matters worse, many developing countries lack ready capital. Without funds, they are less able to get new technologies or build structures to prevent damage from climate change. These countries might want to mitigate future harm from climate change, but the added costs may be just too much to bear.

"They can't get out of their situations. They'll take the brunt of it," says Moser. "A rich country—like ours and much of Europe—will suffer losses, but we can probably cope with that and buy our way out of some of them."

Economic problems fuel political and social unrest. Civil wars and power struggles may topple shaky governments. People with little to lose may also fall victim to the empty promises of terrorists and extremists. When wars break out, the fighting may spill beyond borders and affect other nations around the world.

More-developed countries may be better able to adapt to global climate change, yet they would still feel consequences. Markets would suffer from scarce water resources, impacts on farming and forestry, and other factors. Sea-level rise could cause billions of dollars of damage to coastal areas.

Developed countries would see indirect effects too. Climate disasters could cripple foreign customers' ability to buy goods and services, causing exports to foreign markets to drop off.

Industrialized nations could also expect an influx of immigrants from the hardest-hit countries. Many of those people would probably lack a good education and job skills. A glut of unskilled labor could make unemployment rates skyrocket. Social welfare agencies would be faced with trying to serve a sudden swell in the population.

It is hard to figure out the costs of climate change. After all, estimating effects of climate change involves varying degrees of uncertainty. Matching dollar values to possible losses adds more uncertainty. If all the worst-case scenarios came true, costs would be huge. For the United States alone, various studies indicate that by 2060, market and nonmarket costs could range from $55 billion to $111 billion.

Of course, worldwide costs would be much greater. One estimate by the Organisation for Economic Co-operation and Development estimated the global price tag for climate change costs to be as much as $970 billion.

Insurers worry that climate change could potentially paralyze their industry. Too many catastrophes from hurricanes, landslides, droughts, and other disasters could cause financial ruin if insurers did not have enough reserves to pay for losses they agreed to cover.

In some areas, however, insurers are already raising premiums and reducing coverage. Such action provides financial protection for insurance companies. It can also influence people and businesses to change locations or activities to reduce risks. But some uninsured or underinsured people and businesses may be unable to respond to such changes. If disaster strikes, they may have nothing to fall back on.

From an economic perspective, reducing greenhouse gas emissions would be costly. A wait-and-see approach would put off spending for new technologies and better equipment to cut emissions. A longer timeline would also give companies more time to plan for new capital investments and let them better control costs. They could take steps to cut emissions and, at the same time, they could replace outdated equipment or comply with other regulatory requirements.

Yet the longer people wait, the more climate change will occur. Damages from less than three years of added warming could wipe out all savings from such delay, claims economist William Cline of the Institute for International Economics.

While gaps in scientific knowledge remain, many advocates of action adhere to the "precautionary principle." The principle says governments should not let uncertainty stop them from taking action to protect the environment. Or, more simply: Better safe than sorry.

In 1995, former Vice President Al Gore summed up the feeling:

We ignore these changes at our peril. . . .

> **[W]e must guard against potentially devastating effects, even as we deepen our scientific understanding of these issues through an aggressive research program.**
>
> **[W]hat future generations need is aggressive, measurable and ambitious actions, and not political promises of future actions.**

Ten years later, however, in a 2005 speech at the national Sierra Club Convention, Gore made a more urgent call for action:

> **The warnings about global warming have been extremely clear for a long time. We are facing a global climate crisis. It is deepening. We are entering a period of consequences.**
>
> **The good news is we know what to do. The good news is, we have everything we need now to respond to the challenge of global warming. We have all the technologies we need, more are being developed, and as they become available and become more affordable when produced in scale, they will make it easier to respond. But we should not wait, we cannot wait, we must not wait.**

In 2006 director Davis Guggenheim's documentary *An Inconvenient Truth*, which chronicles Gore's crusade to spread awareness about global warming, was released worldwide. The film not only won the Humanitas Prize and an Oscar, but has also contributed to a green movement that is making eco-friendly products and lifestyles popular. There have been campaigns such as Live Earth, a multi-year endeavor aimed at inspiring individuals, corporations, and governments to actively help solve the climate crises. Live Earth hosted a series of concerts, featuring big names in music and movies, in the summer of 2007 that were covered live by MSN, reaching over 8 million people through 30 million streams.

4

Ongoing Debates

Is the storm of concern about global climate change just a "tempest in a teapot"? Most mainstream scientists say that humans are causing some change in global climate, and that it could present significant problems in decades to come. Yet various issues remain open to debate. Because steps to cut greenhouse gas emissions will undoubtedly have some short-term costs, some scientists and policy-makers also say it is too soon to take action to curb global climate change. What are their arguments?

Are People Really the Problem?

Earth's average temperature is a bit higher than it was a century ago. Since weather naturally varies over time, could the tiny increase have happened on its own? If so, why should people try to fix it?

Harvard astrophysicist Sallie Baliunas says Earth's surface temperature rose roughly 0.7°F (0.4°C) from 1910 to

1940. Yet the biggest increases in greenhouse gas emissions occurred after 1940. Thus, she told the Senate Foreign Relations Committee, "Most of the warming early in this century must have been due to natural causes of climate change."

Variations in the Sun's brightness probably cause some natural climate change. During its eleven-year cycle of magnetic variations, the Sun's radiation output changes. That makes the Sun brighten or fade. "In turn," said Baliunas, "such hypothetical brightness changes could, if large enough, drive significant climate change."

The Sun's electromagnetism and matching energy output vary over longer periods too. For example, the Sun had generally low levels of magnetism from 1640 to 1720, a time period called the Maunder Minimum. A fainter Sun might have been largely responsible for Europe's Little Ice Age at this time. (The world's average global temperature was about 1.8°F (1°C) cooler than it is today.)

Experts differ on how great the Sun's effect on climate change really is. Self-proclaimed greenhouse gas skeptic John L. Daly has argued that solar variability could have caused 90 percent of the last hundred years' warming. Physicists Judith Lean and David Rind disagree and suggest that solar variability explains only half of Earth's warming since 1600. Physicist E. N. Parker at the University of Chicago says the issue is not yet resolved. In other words, scientists should not assume that greenhouse gases are the major factor behind climate change until they understand a lot more about the Sun's role.

Other gaps in scientific knowledge exist too, such as the role of water vapor. Until scientists fully understand natural climate variability, how can anyone say what effect humans have? The inability to "fingerprint" human effects on climate makes it harder to fix the problem.

"For anthropogenic climate change to be 'significant,' it must be as large or larger than natural variability," Massachusetts Institute of Technology meteorologist Richard Lindzen has argued. Even with a lot of background variability, however, a small change caused by greenhouse gases might still have significant impacts on climate.

Other criticisms highlight the limitations of climate models. Models include not only direct effects upon temperature from increased concentrations of greenhouse gases, but also anticipated feedbacks as other parts of the climate system respond to such increases. The Oregon Institute of Science and Medicine contends that most predicted climate effects come from those assumed feedbacks. The group questions whether other scientists should rely on the assumptions about greenhouse effects.

About half of the last century's warming came before 1945, yet greenhouse gas emissions were highest at the end of the century. If greenhouse gases drive warming, argue some scientists, then the largest temperature increase should have coincided with the largest emissions increases.

So why hasn't there been more warming? Sulfate aerosols may explain part of the discrepancy. Aerosols are tiny particles and droplets that are suspended in the atmosphere. Some aerosols spew into the air naturally from events like volcanic eruptions. Many other aerosols come from industrial processes that also add greenhouse gases to the atmosphere. Because aerosols tend to reflect sunlight back into space, says Jeffrey Kiehl at the National Center for Atmospheric Research, they have a temporary cooling effect.

Climatologist Patrick J. Michaels at the University of Virginia has said aerosols do not fully explain why the amount of global warming has been less than models predicted. In his view, the models could be wrong, or other factors may have been at work.

S. Fred Singer of the Science & Environmental Policy Project argues that there are other unknowns too. Scientists do not fully understand mechanisms for how long carbon dioxide stays in the atmosphere. The role of oceans in absorbing the gas is also unclear. Uncertainty still surrounds the crucial role of clouds in climate change. Increased airplane traffic may play a role by putting exhaust gases into the air. Likewise, concrete and buildings in cities often lead to "heat islands," versus other areas where trees and other vegetation have a cooling effect.

Models may even overstate growth in greenhouse gas emissions, claims Danish political scientist Bjørn Lomborg. Actual increases in greenhouse gas emissions may be just fractions of a percent, but a model might round growth rates up to one percent. As the model repeats its calculations, the effect of the rounding gets multiplied, possibly squeezing 120 years of warming into just 70 years. If so, gradual changes in climate would seem much more imminent. Lomborg's ideas have met strong opposition from a large part of the scientific community.

Satellite records add more questions. Since 1979, NASA satellites have measured the atmosphere's temperature worldwide. Actual data show little if any warming in the troposphere, the atmosphere's lower section. Meanwhile, surface measures show an average rise of almost 0.36°F (0.2°C) per decade. This raises questions about the reliability of the surface-temperature record, which is the basis for most climate-model projections.

As a separate matter, at what point do levels of greenhouse gas emissions become dangerous? Shouldn't countries know this before taking costly steps to stop global warming? Without a scientifically sound goal, critics argue, any actions would be purely arbitrary.

While there is much room for disagreement, Eileen

Claussen of the Pew Center on Global Climate Change has said it is a myth to say that people do not really know whether global climate is changing and what is causing it. Citing work by the IPCC's hundreds of scientists around the world, plus the United States' National Academy of Sciences, she says there is "overwhelming scientific consensus" that humans bear some responsibility for Earth's current global warming trend.

Are Predictions of Disaster Overdone?

Even if global climate change is already occurring, some scientists question whether it would really be an awful problem. Patrick J. Michaels at the University of Virginia and Robert Balling at the University of Arizona doubt that warming would make other weather events worse. They claim that arguments about more severe hurricanes are largely speculative. They also question whether tornadoes or thunderstorms would really become more frequent or more severe. Likewise, even if global warming affected the El Niño Southern Oscillation, Michaels and Balling say, there is no evidence that worse weather would result.

What about rising sea levels? Sea levels are already rising in some areas. The most serious problems occur if sea level rises faster than people can adapt to it. Michaels and Balling say that is very unlikely.

Lomborg claims that models overlook the obvious measures that could be taken to combat sea-level rise. Certainly countries would help people set up flood-control programs, including dams, seawalls, and better drainage. When studies of potential disaster assume there will be no such measures, they overestimate the problem. On the other hand, seawalls and other adaptive measures cost money.

Volcanic Chills

On June 12, 1991, Mount Pinatubo in the Philippines erupted, throwing tons of lava, ash, and sulfur dioxide into the air. More than 550 people died, and thousands of homes and farms were destroyed.

Much of the volcano's debris soon settled back to Earth. But tons stayed suspended as aerosols up to 21 miles (35 km) above the ground. The aerosols circled the globe in just three weeks, shadowing more than 40 percent of Earth with their haze. Scientists saw signs of the aerosols as far away as Antarctica and Alaska.

The aerosols in the atmosphere reflected more sunlight back to space, which had a cooling effect on climate. The following year, Earth's average temperature was a whole 1°F (0.6°C) lower.

The effects of that drop were uneven. New Zealand, for example, had a very cold winter and thousands of trees died. At about the same time, the United States had very bad floods. Scientists suspected that the aerosols interfered with the normal functioning of the jet stream, which might have caused heavy rainstorms to remain for a longer time.

History reveals other climate backlashes after volcanic eruptions. Krakatau erupted in Indonesia in 1883. Cold, wet summers swamped Europe for years afterward. After Iceland's Mount Laki erupted in 1783, the United States had a terribly cold winter. There was a huge eruption from Indonesia's Mount Tambora in 1815. In 1816, snow fell on some New England states through June. Meanwhile, France had its worst wine grape harvest in centuries.

Clearly, the volcanic eruptions all occurred naturally. They show that people are not the only force behind Earth's weather. On the other hand, they show how swiftly and dramatically Earth's climate can sometimes respond to even small changes in average temperature. In theory, such changes could follow from either natural or human impacts on the climate.

Many plants, including rice and wheat, should respond positively to increased concentrations of carbon dioxide. With more carbon dioxide in the air, plants should absorb needed amounts of that gas more quickly. As a result, less water would escape from plants' stomata. (Stomata are pores on the undersides of leaves.) In theory, then, plants would use water more efficiently. Irrigation needs could go down, and farmers could enjoy huge harvests.

Studies paid for by the Electric Power Research Institute suggested the United States might even see a small net gain. While some parts of the economy would be hurt by global warming, there would be a huge agricultural boon, according to the studies, which also reported that other damage estimates were overstated. But the studies did not include all ecological consequences of climate change. They relied upon various assumptions to limit losses, and they only looked at the United States.

A report by the Pew Center on Global Climate Change says that, in actuality, the effects on U.S. agriculture may be more mixed. Overall, climate change may bring a small benefit. The Midwest and northern Great Plains may see increased productivity from longer growing seasons, increases in precipitation, and any fertilizing effects from carbon dioxide. The Southeast and southern Great Plains, in contrast, may have lower productivity. There could be varying positive and negative effects on livestock too.

If food production goes up, world hunger might be less of a problem. To the extent that good nutrition lowers disease risks, a warmer world might be a healthier world. Of course, many factors affect whether available food really gets to poor people—how aid money is spent, for example, and whether good distribution networks are in place to get food to hungry people.

Also, other parts of the world are likely to have more

serious drought problems than the United States. All crops do not respond as well to higher carbon dioxide levels, either. In short, farmers in other countries could still be hurt by global climate change.

Questions about Health Effects

Although some scientists say climate change will mean more heat-related deaths in the summer, Michaels and Balling argue that extreme cold kills twice as many people as extreme heat. Snow, ice, and hail cause more traffic accidents, which cost lives. People also die of exposure during cold weather, especially poor and homeless people. In contrast, heat-related deaths dropped dramatically in the twentieth century, thanks to air conditioning. Of course, air conditioning requires electricity—which often uses fossil fuels like coal, and in turn adds greenhouse gases to the atmosphere.

When heat-related deaths do occur, deciding exactly what caused such deaths can be difficult. Suppose that someone has a heart attack during a hot spell. Suppose further that the person had a pre-existing heart condition. Did the heat really cause the death? Sometimes death rates drop for the few days after a heat spell finally breaks. That suggests that during the heat spell some deaths may have happened anyway. (On the other hand, since everyone will die someday, anything that moves that time up is a cause of death.)

Some scientists also question whether warmer weather would really drive up rates of malaria and other diseases. European temperatures were generally cooler during the Little Ice Age that followed the Middle Ages. Yet malaria was still a serious health problem in England during the coldest period. Better medical techniques and public health programs in the 1800s finally helped fight malaria.

More recently, malaria rates have surged in areas of East Africa. Simon Hay and his colleagues in the University of Oxford's department of zoology argued in the journal *Nature* that the affected regions had not yet experienced significant climate changes. "We hope these findings will help focus attention back to the real and immediate problem of anti-malarial drug resistance, rather than potential future problems that climate change may bring," announced Hay. Other scientists, such as Johns Hopkins University's Jonathan Patz, questioned the research team's use of climate-model data in their study.

Even if warming made potential areas of infection expand, public health practices and modern medical knowledge might keep epidemics from spreading too much. Rather than trying to change the weather, it might be better to build better public health programs worldwide. That would address not just disease related to climate change, but also the awful epidemics that already kill millions every year.

Too Expensive?

Some groups say the price tag for cutting greenhouse gas emissions is just too high. According to a report by the conservative Heritage Foundation, adhering to the 1997 Kyoto Protocol could slash the United States' productivity by up to $400 billion. Gas prices could rise by 30 to 50 percent. Overall energy costs could jump more than 80 percent. Meanwhile, the job market would shrink. Americans' standard of living could fall by about 15 percent.

Similar dire predictions have come from Charles River Associates, Wharton Econometric Forecasting Associates, and other groups. Under worst-case scenarios, cutting greenhouse gas emissions could cost individual American households an average of $2,000 or more.

The heaviest burdens would fall on the poor and middle class. People could face long lines at gas stations and higher energy costs. Many people remember the 1970s' energy crisis and do not want to face that again.

And extensive spending to cut greenhouse gas emissions might not result in a payoff. Even with emissions limits, it could take decades or even a century before any minor reversal in climate changes occurred. Meanwhile, critics like Thomas Gale Moore of the Hoover Institution argue that remedial measures would cripple America's economy.

For this reason, Marlo Lewis of the Competitive Enterprise Institute criticized a 2002 Senate bill that called for cuts in power-plant emissions. Power companies might cut emissions, but they would pass the costs on to consumers. Residential electricity costs could go up 25 percent by 2010. Even if the Clean Power Act became law, said Lewis, it might only avoid 0.02°F (0.013°C) of global warming during the next century—an infinitesimal change.

Is it really worth the time and effort to spend so much to mitigate global climate change? People who don't believe global climate change is a problem obviously do not think it is worthwhile to prevent disasters that may never happen.

Indeed, as some industrialized countries cut their emissions, other countries' emissions are likely to go up even more. On the one hand, the total level of greenhouse gases would be much higher without any cuts. On the other hand, is it right to require some countries to cut their emissions and possibly lower their standard of living while other nations put more greenhouse gases into the air?

Other policymakers think too many questions remain unanswered to justify substantial cuts in greenhouse gas emissions. In late 2002, for example, the Bush administration announced plans for more intensive studies on climate change. Those studies will provide more in-depth knowledge on various issues, yet scientific knowledge is almost never perfect. Thus, there may never be enough proof to persuade some critics to take action on global climate change.

Of course, global climate change is not the only policy issue that needs attention. Many wants and needs vie for limited resources. Some policymakers prefer to spend money to address other social problems that seem more real and immediate to them than the chance that the climate could change sometime in the future.

On the other hand, studies can overestimate costs in various ways. They can assume that industries will have to take the most drastic measures to reduce greenhouse gases, instead of less burdensome alternatives. They can omit economic benefits associated with emissions cuts, such as related reductions in pollution or growth in alternative energy technologies. They can make assumptions about higher future spending and interest rates that unfairly inflate estimated costs.

Why Not Adapt?

People have been adapting to climate change for thousands of years. Why couldn't we just adapt to future climate change? For people who think global climate change is not really a serious problem, that would be the most efficient solution.

For example, coastal areas already face serious hurricane and flood risks. Inland areas suffer from droughts, thunderstorms, and tornadoes. If existing preventive measures were enhanced, that would make any human-caused climate change in the future less disastrous.

While adaptive measures may reduce some harmful effects of global climate change, those measures themselves can cost substantial amounts of money. In other words, adapta-

VOLCANIC DUST STAYED SUSPENDED IN EARTH'S ATMOSPHERE AFTER
MT. PINATUBO'S ERUPTION IN 1991. VARIOUS REGIONS AROUND THE
GLOBE HAD NOTICEABLE DROPS IN AVERAGE TEMPERATURE AND
CHANGES IN PRECIPITATION PATTERNS THE FOLLOWING YEAR.

tion does not eliminate the costs of global climate change. It is merely another category of costs related to global warming.

Also, adaptive measures may not be enough to deal with the potential harm of global climate change. Climate changes related to greenhouse gas emissions may well occur sooner than people can adapt to changed conditions with enhanced shoreline protection or other measures. Adaptive measures cannot eliminate all risks either. Indeed, hurricanes presently cause serious damage even in parts of the United States that are relatively well-equipped to deal with them.

5
Treaty Time

"[C]hange in the Earth's climate and its adverse effects are a common concern of humankind," according to the 1992 United Nations Framework Convention on Climate Change (UNFCCC). In 1997, the parties to that treaty negotiated the Kyoto Protocol. The treaty calls for countries on a list known as Annex I to cut greenhouse gas emissions. But the United States has not ratified it. What is all the fuss about?

1992: Countries Agree to Address Global Warming

After the IPCC's 1990 report, people from 150 countries talked about what to do. By June 1992, they agreed on the United Nations Framework Convention on Climate Change. The U.S. Senate ratified the UNFCCC treaty later that same year. As of early 2003, 188 governments had formally become parties to the UNFCCC.

This treaty's goal is to prevent dangerous human

interference with Earth's climate. However, the agreement did not define "dangerous." That issue was left for future political and scientific talks. But UNFCCC did spell out some general principles.

The precautionary principle is a primary concept in the UNFCCC. Basically, it says lack of scientific certainty is no excuse for putting off action if serious or irreversible damage is a threat.

When it comes to taking action, the UNFCCC says "equity" requires that countries should have "common but differentiated responsibilities." In other words, all countries agreed to some general duties. For example, all would share information about their greenhouse gas emissions and all would have some national programs for dealing with climate change.

But some countries would have more responsibilities—the forty-one countries listed by the UNFCCC as industrialized nations. They include the United States, Canada, the United Kingdom, France, Japan, Spain, and Switzerland. They also include countries changing over from communism, such as the Russian Federation, the Czech Republic, Poland, and Slovakia. In general, Annex I countries would adopt national policies to cut greenhouse gas emissions back to 1990 baselines. The UNFCCC did not spell out how they would do that.

While countries that were not listed in Annex I had to make some reports, the UNFCCC imposed no duty on them to cut greenhouse gas emissions. Of course, developing countries' emissions still go into the air. But the UNFCCC's distinction between Annex I and non–Annex I countries rested more on policy considerations than on science.

"The argument from the 'south' is that the first-world [countries] got their 'first world' status by using large amounts of fossil fuel energy per capita, and ought to go first in putting limits on their use," explained F. Sherwood

Rowland of the University of California, Irvine. First-world countries, such as the United States and western European nations, are richer and more industrialized than other nations. If those countries go first in cutting greenhouse gas emissions, third-world developing countries have a better chance of catching up economically. This argument assumes that economic growth will continue to be linked to higher levels of fossil fuel usage.

Historically, too, developing nations have had far lower greenhouse gas emissions per person than the industrialized countries. As a matter of fairness, developing countries can argue that they have a right to higher per capita emissions. As of 2006, for example, China's per capita greenhouse gas emissions was about one-sixth of that of the United States.

The UNFCCC was a big step forward because it stated the world's concern about global climate change. After the treaty became effective, the parties met each year to share information, but something more was needed.

In 1995, UNFCCC party representatives held their annual meeting in Berlin, Germany. Many people felt the UNFCCC treaty needed more substance if greenhouse gas emissions were to go down. Countries decided to develop a supplemental agreement. It would place duties on Annex I countries to cut greenhouse gas emissions to specific levels. The parties planned to hammer out details of an agreement at a December 1997 conference in Kyoto, Japan.

Countdown to Kyoto

Leaders of the world's leading industrialized countries met in June 1997 at the Earth Summit +5 special session of the United Nations. Previously, other countries had seen the United States as stalling on the issue of global climate change. Now the Clinton administration wanted to change its image. Addressing other countries' delegates in New York, President Bill Clinton said:

> **The science is clear and compelling. We humans are changing the global climate. . . . We will work with our people—and we will bring to the Kyoto conference in December a strong American commitment to realistic and binding limits that will significantly reduce our emissions of greenhouse gases.**

Other countries probably were pleased with President Clinton's comments, but the remarks had the reverse effect among business leaders and politicians at home.

In response, the U.S. Senate passed Senate Resolution 98. It warned President Clinton not to agree to any treaty to cut the United States' emissions unless developing countries also had limits. Otherwise, the resolution said, there could be "serious harm to the United States economy, including significant job loss, trade disadvantages, increased energy and consumer costs, or any combination thereof. . ."

Passed by a vote of 95–0, the resolution reflected broad support from both Democrats and Republicans. Basically, politicians feared that emissions limits would mean added costs for American businesses but not for businesses in developing countries. Foreign countries would be able to produce goods more cheaply, possibly costing American companies money and American workers jobs.

President Clinton had said unequivocally that the United States would be a leader on the global climate change issue and would agree to cut its greenhouse gas emissions. Even before the Kyoto conference opened, United States negotiators were at a disadvantage.

The Kyoto Protocol

The Kyoto conference called for industrialized countries to cut greenhouse gas emissions. At first, the Americans did not want to budge below 1990 emissions levels. The European Union wanted more cuts in emissions. German foreign minister Klaus Kinkel said that by 2010, countries should cut greenhouse gas emissions 15 percent below 1990 levels. Great Britain's environment minister, Michael Meacher, wanted 20 percent cuts. Developing countries demanded even more—as much as about one-third below 1990 levels by 2020.

Negotiators could not agree how much to cut emissions, so Vice President Al Gore went to Japan to discuss the reductions. Finally, the United States agreed to a 7 percent average greenhouse gas emissions cut to be achieved between 2008 and 2012. The European Union agreed to an 8 percent cut. On average, industrial countries' greenhouse gas emissions would go down about 5 percent. Countries not listed in Annex I had no binding duty to cut emissions.

Countries were free to choose how to reduce their own greenhouse gas emissions. For example, requiring permits could limit companies' emissions in a country. Such a system already operates in the United States to limit industrial pollution under the Clean Air Act and the Clean Water Act. Alternatively, higher taxes might curb nonessential use of gasoline, electricity, and other sources of greenhouse gas emissions. A country could also reward energy-efficient activities or early replacement of less-efficient capital equipment. Any or all of these strategies could help reduce overall emissions.

Conservation of forests and other carbon "sinks" could also count toward emission reductions. Burning forests and grasslands for development or farming releases carbon from vegetation into the air. In contrast, plant growth essentially pulls carbon dioxide from the air and ties up the carbon in the plant's structure. By virtue of their size, trees fix the most carbon in place. Thus, conserving land for carbon sinks could not entirely relieve countries of their duty to cut emissions, but it might make compliance easier.

Meeting the Kyoto Protocol's obligations entirely within one's own borders could still be costly. Many industrial plants in countries with strong environmental programs already pollute less and are more efficient than average facilities in other countries. How much more could those countries cut back without serious economic harm? To make things easier, the Kyoto Protocol offered three choices.

Emissions trading is one major option. Countries that must lower their emissions can make deals with each other. A country that thinks its 2012 emissions will be below its target could sell any emissions credits to another Annex I country.

Emissions trading gives potential windfalls to countries like the Russian Federation and the Ukraine. The Kyoto Protocol set targets for both of these countries at 100 percent of their 1990 emissions. In other words, they would not have to go below 1990 emissions levels. Since the Soviet Union collapsed, however, both of these countries (which were once part of the Soviet Union), had economic setbacks. Their economies are unlikely to get back to 1990 levels soon, so they would not need their full allotments. Selling the credits for the extra emissions might yield billions of dollars.

That would be a good deal for Russia and the Ukraine. It may not be such a bad deal for other countries, either. Countries with healthier economies would not want to slow their own industrial growth. They would pay so they could keep their own power plants and factories going at full production.

The clean-development mechanism was another way to ease the burdens of compliance. An industrialized nation could pay for a project to reduce greenhouse gas emissions in a developing country. The project could cost less for the industrialized country than further emissions cuts at home. The developing country would get more efficient, less-polluting technology. Overall, emissions of greenhouse gases would be lower.

The Kyoto Protocol also let parties make agreements with each other to jointly reduce their emissions. Joint implementation lets participating countries decide among themselves what makes the most sense for them to meet their combined targets. It also gets rid of some duplication.

With these provisions in place, the conference adopted the Kyoto Protocol on December 11, 1997. Representatives of eighty-four countries signed it during 1998 and 1999. Next, individual governments would have to formally ratify or accede to the treaty. The Kyoto Protocol would become effective only when ratified by Annex I countries with at least 55 percent of that group's total 1990 carbon dioxide emissions.

Many issues remained open. Just how would emissions trading work? Who would approve and oversee any trades? Who would decide whether a clean-development mechanism was a good idea? What sinks would count as credits? How would countries know if other nations carried out their agreements?

To Ratify or Not to Ratify

The United States signed the Kyoto Protocol on November 12, 1998. Under the Constitution, the treaty could not bind the United States without Senate approval. Yet President Clinton never sent the Kyoto Protocol to the Senate for ratification. The Republican-controlled Senate would have voted against it. Given the 95–0 vote on Senate Resolution 98, even a Democrat-led Senate would likely have rejected the treaty.

President George W. Bush effectively slammed the door on the Kyoto Protocol. Several senators had asked the president where he stood on global climate change. In a March 2001 letter, he replied:

> **As you know, I oppose the Kyoto Protocol because it exempts 80 percent of the world, including major population centers such as China and India, from compliance, and would cause serious harm to the U.S. economy. The Senate's [1997] vote, 95–0, shows that there is a clear consensus that the Kyoto Protocol is an unfair and ineffective means of addressing global climate change concerns.**

In February 2002, the president announced his "Clear Skies" initiative, which called for reductions in mercury and other air pollutants. On the subject of climate change, the president called for an 18 percent reduction in "greenhouse gas intensity" by 2012. This means that the country would emit fewer gases per unit of its economic productivity. That would be the equivalent of 70 million fewer cars on the road. Yet the total amount of emissions could still go up if economic activity increased.

The Clear Skies initiative relied mainly on voluntary programs. It did not call for mandatory emissions cuts such as the United States would have had under the terms of the Kyoto Protocol. The President defended his decision:

> **The approach taken under the Kyoto Protocol would have required the United States to make deep and**

immediate cuts in our economy to meet an arbitrary target. It would have cost our economy up to $400 billion and we would have lost 4.9 million jobs.

As President of the United States, charged with safeguarding the welfare of the American people and American workers, I will not commit our nation to an unsound international treaty that will throw millions of our citizens out of work.

Indeed, the Kyoto Protocol's target of a 7 percent emissions cut from 1990 levels loomed large. The United States

DEMONSTRATORS AT A SUMMIT IN RIO DE JANEIRO PROTEST THE UNITED STATES' FAILURE TO RATIFY AND COMPLY WITH THE KYOTO PROTOCOL IN JUNE 2002.

economy—and its emissions—had grown since 1990. Economics advisors hoped some growth would continue through 2010. Greenhouse gas emissions probably would increase as the economy grew. To obey the Kyoto Protocol, the United States might have to cut its projected emissions by 25 or even 30 percent.

Just a few months later, the U.S. Environmental Protection Agency issued its Third National Communication under the UNFCCC. The report described America's voluntary programs to address climate change. At the same time, the report said that global climate change was a real and serious problem that could cause serious economic and environmental losses within America. Despite that, President Bush came out against the treaty. "The Kyoto treaty would severely damage the United States economy, and I don't accept that," he said.

The president's political foes denounced his decision not to join the Kyoto Protocol. An opinion piece by former Vice President Al Gore, called "The Selling of An Energy Policy," ran on the editorial page of *The New York Times* on Earth Day 2002.

President Bush's position outraged environmental groups too. "Bush Caves in to Fossil Fuel Industry," announced a Greenpeace press release. "When big business banged on the White House door, President Bush made a policy U-turn that will haunt our children," said Carl Pope of the Sierra Club.

The United States had played a major role in meetings that led up to the Kyoto Protocol. "To simply throw it out is basically throwing out ten years of negotiations in which the United States was involved until the very last minute," said Susi Moser of the Union of Concerned Scientists. "They got pretty much everything they wanted, and then they walked away."

The Kyoto Protocol Moves Ahead

Despite the United States' position, other countries moved forward. The Kyoto Protocol does not need universal approval. No one country—not even a major source of greenhouse gas emissions—can veto it. It could become effective when ratified by at least fifty-five countries, including at least enough Annex I countries to represent 55 percent of their 1990 emissions, as listed in Annex I to the UNFCCC.

By June 2007, 174 countries had formally accepted the Kyoto Protocol. The ratifying group's industrialized countries included Japan, Slovakia, and those in the European Union. Many developing countries joined too, such as Lesotho, Nicaragua, Guatemala, Paraguay, and Senegal.

The protocol went into effect on February 16, 2005 with enough Annex I parties to represent 61.6 percent of their collective 1990 emissions. The U.S. was not one of them. The Kyoto Protocol binds only the countries that have ratified or accepted it.

Meanwhile, parties to the UNFCCC meet each year to talk about how emissions trading will work, credits for carbon "sinks," and other issues. Slowly but surely, countries are working out the details.

Because it remains a party to the UNFCCC, the United States can still send representatives to meetings. Since it still produces the world's largest share of greenhouse gas emissions, America's bargaining power may diminish if it stays out of the Kyoto Protocol. Other countries may be less willing to agree to the United States' positions if America will not accept restrictions on its emissions.

That change in bargaining power might affect other issues, such as trade agreements or military defense. Other countries may agree with the United States on such topics, but they may not want to help out if they think the United States will not act for the good of the planet.

Likewise, American companies could face trouble marketing lower-emissions technologies abroad. Faced with a choice between sellers, other countries might prefer companies whose governments have agreed to the Kyoto Protocol.

Fatally Flawed, or a Fundamental First Step?

Could the Kyoto Protocol really curb global warming? While scientists know a lot about global climate change, uncertainty still surrounds many issues. Among other things, what level of carbon dioxide emissions is "safe"? And what effect would an average reduction of 5 percent of emissions have? Without a clear benefit in mind, policymakers may well wonder whether or not to commit substantial resources to any emissions-reduction project.

Not even its biggest promoters say the Kyoto Protocol will reverse or even halt global climate change. Yet environmental groups and concerned governments see it as an important first step.

"It provides an institutional framework," says Moser. "It's a door opener. It's an institutional structure that allows us to move forward with much more stringent emissions controls that eventually we will need."

Many governments, including that of the United States, spent a lot of time working out the terms of the Kyoto Protocol. Before President Bush announced his outright opposition to the treaty, Christie Whitman, then-administrator of the U.S. Environmental Protection Agency, warned:

> **The Kyoto Protocol is the only game in town in their eyes. There is a real fear in the international community that if the U.S. is not willing to discuss the issue within the framework of Kyoto the whole thing will fall apart. They feel that they can move ahead toward their goals on their own, but would need the U.S. to really get things done.**

President Bush said cost was a big factor in saying no to the Kyoto Protocol. Based on different cost estimates, compliance would have cost the economy as much as $400 billion or more, a large sum even in the best of economic times. America's economy had already dipped slightly after Bush became president.

The Kyoto Protocol's short time frame for compliance was another issue. In theory, a longer time frame would let companies wait until equipment needed replacing before spending a lot on new technologies. More time might also bring even better, more efficient improvements in emissions-reduction technology.

Without deadlines, however, countries might not act in a timely way to cut greenhouse gas emissions. Just as students often put off large projects until right before the due date, governments can procrastinate.

The concept that more time means a more efficient solution is also open to debate. Many coal-fired power plants are already rather old and need upgrading, noted Moser. If so, companies may not be wholly honest when they argue that cutting greenhouse gas emissions will force the replacement of large amounts of capital equipment. If one is going to replace equipment, why not use the latest technology instead of waiting for something better to come along?

Whether equipment is old or new, companies must comply with existing environmental laws. For example, industries in the United States will still have to reduce emissions of mercury, sulfur dioxide, and nitrous oxide. In Moser's view, it is actually more cost effective to cut carbon dioxide emissions at the same time that industry reduces levels of those other pollutants. On the other hand, costs for reducing different kinds of emissions can vary significantly, so that the issue may not be as simple as regulating just one more pollutant.

Fairness is a separate issue. Based on 1990 levels, the United States was the world's biggest source of carbon dioxide emissions. According to the UNFCCC, the United States produced just over 36 percent of calculated carbon dioxide emissions—5 million metric tons. From other countries' perspectives, the world's greenhouse gas giant should certainly cut back its emissions.

But the Kyoto Protocol puts mandatory limits only on the countries listed in Annex I. During the next several decades, China, India, Indonesia, Brazil, and Nigeria will probably increase their share of global greenhouse gas emissions. Yet these countries do not have any duties under the Kyoto Protocol. They also have not indicated that they will accept such limits in the near future.

The position of countries such as India and China under the Kyoto Protocol fuels fears that American companies could be at a competitive disadvantage. Indeed, any environmental gains from cutting emissions could be more than offset by developing countries' growing output of greenhouse gases. Without assurance that foreign competitors will face similar emissions limits (and therefore economic limits), many companies will not want to make costly changes in how they do business.

On the other hand, developing countries can claim

that they want a chance to "catch up" to the industrialized world. For now, they would rather feed their people and boost their economies. Most developing nations are likely to resist any limits on greenhouse gas emissions.

Nonetheless, some developing countries are taking steps to reduce or avoid greenhouse gas emissions as their economies grow. The Pew Center on Global Climate Change reports that programs in Brazil, China, India, Turkey, South Africa, and Mexico have already lowered greenhouse gas emissions by 300 million tons annually.

Moving Forward in the International Arena

Even without the Kyoto Protocol, the United States government is taking some action. It has been negotiating separate treaties, or side deals, with other governments.

In 2002, the United States and Australia announced the U.S.–Australia Climate Action Partnership. While neither country has ratified the Kyoto Protocol, the countries' current agreement deals with emissions offsets. Under that concept, measures to protect forests, grasslands, and other carbon sinks can count against emissions. It also addresses projects for new technologies that yield lower greenhouse gas emissions.

The United States has also worked on an agreement with India in which it will help India add energy-saving technologies, like fuel cells and solar power, that will help lower India's emissions. The United States will also provide help with climate modeling and weather forecasting. The U.S. government has also met with other countries, including Italy and Japan, about emissions issues.

Such bilateral agreements resemble parts of the Kyoto Protocol on emissions offsets and clean-development

Debate about the Bottom Line

President George W. Bush cited a $400 billion price tag as a main reason for rejecting the Kyoto Protocol. Would compliance really cost that much?

Before the United States signed the Kyoto Protocol in 1998, Janet Yellen, the head of President Clinton's Council of Economic Advisors, told a congressional committee that the average household might pay just an extra $70 to $110 a year. People might not even pay that much if electric utility deregulation spurred greater competition and lowered prices.

Yellen used best-case scenarios. She also assumed that America could satisfy about 85 percent of its obligations under the Kyoto Protocol by emissions trading. Subsequent negotiations have limited how much of their emissions targets countries can trade away. Clean-development mechanisms, carbon sinks, and other techniques to offset actual emissions likewise will have limits.

The $400 billion estimate came from a later study by the U.S. Energy Information Administration. That group assumed the United States would have to meet more than 80 percent of its emissions cuts at home with costs per household of more than $3,500. While other studies' totals were smaller, costs could still be more than $200 billion.

Environmental groups disagree with those studies and say that the Kyoto Protocol would not cripple the country. Indeed, a 2001 report by the World Wildlife Fund said the United States could meet its emissions target and still save $50 billion per year. Part of the money could come from auctions of carbon-emissions permits, while tax credits could produce other savings. People could also save money with more efficient vehicles and appliances, as well as by using renewable energy sources. By 2020, annual savings could grow to $135 billion.

So, who's right? A lot depends on how one counts costs. It also depends on what substitutions are available for emissions-intensive technology. Another substantial factor is how much savings from reduced pollution, innovative technologies, and other sources can offset any costs.

The time scale involved in global climate change complicates economic estimates even more. Usually, economists consider time periods of twenty to thirty years to be long term. In contrast, it can take a century or more before people experience some of the effects of global climate change. The timeline for reaping the benefits of emissions-cutting measures can likewise span generations. When economists assume a steady interest and discount rate to account for the value of money, their analyses may have an inherent bias one way or the other. An alternative approach may be to account somehow for anticipated variations in value of money over time.

mechanisms, but these agreements do not restrict the United States' emissions.

With or without the Kyoto Protocol, international negotiations on global climate change will continue on various fronts. Other countries will be watching what the United States does at home to slow the growth of, or to cut, greenhouse gas emissions.

6

What Happens Next?

"Addressing global climate change will require a sustained effort over many generations," President George W. Bush said in early 2002. Later that year, the U.S. Commerce Department announced plans for a four-year program of in-depth studies on climate change. Among other things, the government's strategic study plan called for more detailed analysis of carbon dioxide and methane buildup from sources in North America, as well as of how different ecosystems bind up carbon from the atmosphere. Other studies will look at issues such as the role of clouds and climate feedbacks relating to water vapor; the effect of aerosols on climate change; better understanding of the carbon cycle; and feedbacks in the polar regions that could affect present climate model predictions. Other parts of the strategic plan focus on how climate models could be improved to reduce uncertainties.

Some interest groups and policymakers would prefer to postpone substantial actions to cut greenhouse gas emissions until all answers are in. Meanwhile, other interest groups and policymakers at both the state and federal levels want the United States to move forward on curbing emissions even as studies progress. In their view, there is already sufficient consensus that global climate change is happening and that human activities are a cause. Because it is a large industrial country, the United States' actions can make a difference.

By far, the biggest share of the United States' greenhouse gas emissions comes from burning fossil fuels, with electric power plants and automobiles contributing the most. To cut carbon dioxide emissions, citizens would have to pursue any or all of three approaches:

- cut energy and transportation uses that depend on fossil fuels;

- use fossil fuels much more efficiently than they do today;

- use alternative energy sources for electricity and transportation.

Competing Interests

Many environmentalists, consumers, and government groups say they want lower greenhouse gas emissions. Different groups place different priorities on the issue, however. For example, some environmental activist organizations give the issue top priority with little room for compromise.

Other groups take a more moderate approach, emphasizing reduction of greenhouse gases consistent with economic growth. Many consumers would probably say they feel that way too.

How Long Would It Take to Reduce Greenhouse-Gas Buildup?

Forcing Agent	Approximate Removal Times	Climate Forcing Up to the Year 2000
GREENHOUSE GASES		
Carbon Dioxide	>100 years	1.3 to 1.5
Methane	10 years	0.5 to 0.7
Tropospheric Ozone	10–100 days	0.25 to 0.75
Nitrous Oxide	100 years	0.1 to 0.3
Perfluorocarbon Compounds (Including SF$_6$)	>1,000 years	0.01
FINE AEROSOLS		
Sulfate	10 days	-0.3 to -1.0
Black Carbon	10 days	0.1 to 0.8

EMISSIONS THAT CONTRIBUTE TO CLIMATE CHANGE CAN STAY IN THE ATMOSPHERE A LONG TIME. "APPOXIMATE REMOVAL TIMES" MEANS THE PERIODS NEEDED FOR MOST OF AN EMISSION TO LEAVE THE ATMOSPHERE. FOR EXAMPLE, AN APPROXIMATE REMOVAL TIME OF ONE HUNDRED YEARS WOULD BE NEEDED TO REMOVE ABOUT 63 PERCENT OF AN EMISSION OF NITROUS OXIDE. "CLIMATE FORCING UP TO THE YEAR 2000" REPRESENTS THE APPROXIMATE ADDED HEAT ENERGY IN THE ATMOSPHERE FROM DIFFERENT TYPES OF EMISSIONS.

Source: U.S. Environmental Protection Agency, U.S. Climate Action Report—2002: Third National Communication of the United States of America Under the United Nations Framework Convention on Climate Change, 2002, p. 252.

In the short run, some labor groups might object to cutting greenhouse gases if they thought such measures would cost jobs. A policy that cut demand for a certain type of energy or product, like coal, could indeed displace workers in some industries, but worker-training programs could address part of that problem. If workers knew they could still get a job, they would be more likely to support measures to cut emissions.

Company directors are in a different position because they have a legal duty to make money for shareholders. Some companies have most of their assets and production tied up in older technologies that cause more emissions than newer technologies.

Coal companies, for example, make money by mining and selling coal. They stand to lose profits if people switch to other energy sources. Electric utilities often want to maximize present profits. To do this, they may want to put off spending for equipment that could lower emissions, since that would lower their immediate profit margin.

Some companies and groups will indeed lose out if the United States moves away from its heavy fossil-fuel consumption. Such interests play a substantial part in the lack of enthusiasm for adapting alternative energy on a large-scale basis.

On the other hand, many worthwhile innovations draw money away from pre-existing activities. Indeed, some companies may be able to make more money by investing in renewable energy technologies. Both BP and Royal Dutch/Shell are large petroleum companies that have also branched out into solar and wind power. By 2002, BP had become the leading maker of photovoltaic cells.

A Power Struggle

Sparks fly when the global climate change debate focuses on electricity. Electric power plants account for about 40 percent of the carbon dioxide emitted within the United States. Coal-fired electric power plants emit over 85 percent of that carbon dioxide, with natural gas and petroleum-powered plants making up the remainder. Coal-powered plants also emit over 90 percent of the energy industry's nitrous oxide, another greenhouse gas. Environmental groups also complain about other types of pollution from these plants, such as chemicals that produce smog, soot, and mercury pollution.

Electric utilities claim that they have already substantially cut greenhouse gas emissions. On a per unit basis, utilities generally produce far less pollution than they did decades ago. However, the Natural Resources Defense Council claims that power plant emissions in 2000 were actually 25 percent higher than 1990 levels.

The biggest cuts would probably come as a result of a shift away from coal as a power source. Both the coal industry and the electric industry have resisted that approach. But some environmental groups think coal-powered plants are outdated and prefer cleaner technologies.

Hydroelectric power has almost no bad effects on human health or global climate change. Presently, just under 10 percent of America's generating plants use water power. Expanding hydroelectric capability is certainly one way to create more electrical capacity. On the other hand, plant construction could raise concerns about potential habitat damage and plant operation could alter water levels. Power companies would have to take care not to hurt species that live in and depend on rivers.

Nuclear power likewise emits almost no greenhouse gases. And there are few human health effects, as long as people run the plant safely. However, nuclear power plant accidents have happened in the past.

In 1979, the water cooling system for the nuclear reactor at the Three Mile Island plant in Pennsylvania malfunctioned.

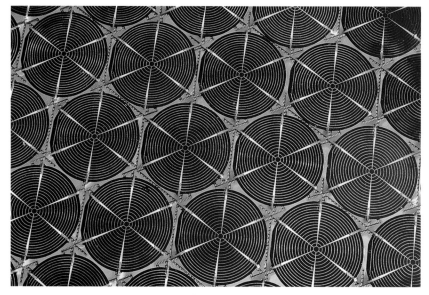

PHOTOVOLTAICS (SOLAR POWER) WORK BY CONVERTING LIGHT FROM THE SUN INTO ELECTRICITY. PHOTOVOLTAICS ARE ENVIRONMENTALLY SAFE BUT COSTLY COMPARED TO EXISTING MEANS OF PRODUCING ELECTRICITY.

By the time the workers got everything under control, part of a reactor core had melted, and radiation had leaked. People still debate whether the radiation or stress related to the accident caused various cancer cases in surrounding communities. Meanwhile, during the two decades following the incident, power companies built no new nuclear plants in the United States. Besides safety concerns, environmental groups also worry about the lack of permanent storage facilities for radioactive waste, which remains toxic for thousands of years.

Despite concerns, both nuclear power and hydroelectric power have had relatively good track records within the United States. In the future, they may produce a bigger share of America's electricity. Meanwhile, government, environmental groups, and even industry are looking at alternative ways to produce the power that America needs. While such technologies play a small part in power generation in the United States today, they could play a substantial role in the future.

Alternative Energy Technologies

Photovoltaics, or solar power, convert sunlight into electricity. Since the Sun will keep shining for billions of years, photovoltaics rely on a renewable energy supply and do not release greenhouse gases or other pollutants into the air.

When light shines on a photovoltaic cell, electricity is produced. Positively charged photons in the light cause electrons to jump from one atom to the next within the cell. The jumping electrons leave "holes" that attract electrons from neighboring atoms. This flow of electrons is an electric current.

Photovoltaic cells only make electricity when the Sun shines. For nighttime power, stand-alone photovoltaics can store power in a battery. Because connection to an electric grid is not required, photovoltaics potentially can make electricity anywhere. As John Thornton of the National Renewable Energy Laboratory (NREL) noted, "Two billion people in the world do not have any electricity at all." Thus, solar power is good news for the world's developing countries.

Solar energy can be an important add-on for existing power grids. Photovoltaic cells tend to work most efficiently in the afternoon hours. As luck would have it, that coincides with utilities' peak demand periods. That's when most people turn up the air conditioning and other electric appliances.

"The output of photovoltaics in most utilities around the U.S. matches their peak load profile pretty well," explains

John Benner at the NREL, "so you can mix photovoltaic power in with the other generating capacity that the utility has."

Because peak generating capacity tends to be most expensive for utilities, photovoltaics can compete effectively with other choices. Combining solar power with existing power grids can also make solar power practical for areas that might not be able to use it year round. Alaska, for example, has frigid, dark winters, but parts of the state get twenty hours of sunlight a day in the summer. That's just when the tourist and canning industries boost demand for electricity.

If solar energy is such a great idea, why don't people use it more? The answer is cost. Compared with the rest of the world, U.S. citizens pay very little for electricity and gasoline, since prices for coal and fossil fuels are relatively cheap. In some areas, coal-generated electricity may cost just two cents per kilowatt-hour, while electricity from solar power may cost ten times as much.

Most photovoltaic cells today are made of semiconductors, such as crystalline silicon. The more precise the crystal lattice is within the material, the more efficiently it can perform. However, those types of semiconductors are expensive to produce.

Researchers have recently developed some "thin-film" photovoltaic cells from less-expensive materials. An example is amorphous silicon. (Amorphous here means that the material is more glasslike and lacks an elaborately structured lattice.) The cheaper material could help bring the cost of photovoltaics down. First, however, scientists must improve the thin-film cells' efficiency enough to make them practical.

Wind power is another alternative. Basically, mechanical energy from spinning windmill blades powers electrical generators in attached turbines. Transformers step up the voltage and send electricity down the line to distributors. Like solar power, wind power does not emit greenhouse gases and other pollutants.

But wind power does not work everywhere. Spinning turbines are loud, making around 50 decibels of noise, and some people feel that long rows of windmills are unsightly. Homeowners may not want wind farms close by. Also, because the wind does not blow all the time, users would need battery storage or supplemental power.

Nonetheless, wind farms in California, Texas, Iowa, Oregon, and elsewhere can significantly supplement conventional power generation. Iowa's Waverly Light and Power installed its first utility-scale wind turbine in 1993. By 2002, the state's 350 wind turbines were capable of generating more than 500 megawatts of electricity, enough to light 5 million 100-watt lightbulbs. In Texas, Dallas-based TXU Energy began buying power from wind farms for a cost of about five cents per kilowatt-hour, a rate that is competitive with other forms of power.

Hydrogen fuel cells may help power businesses and homes, as well as energy-smart automobiles. In New York City, for example, the fifty-one-story Condé Nast Building at 4 Times Square uses both fuel cells and photovoltaic cells to generate on-site electricity. Yet power and other environmentally friendly features still cost around $14 million a year for the building at Times Square, which is nicknamed the Green Giant.

Geothermal power is another possible alternative energy source. Heat from hot springs can warm buildings as their steam turns turbines to make electricity. Wave and tidal power are also possibilities. These technologies' usefulness depends on geography. Power plants also have to be constructed in a way that prevents damage to wildlife and fish habitats.

Biomass burning is yet another option. Burning non-fossil organic matter can cut down on fossil-fuel consumption. It can even provide a good way to use wastes. Biomass burning still produces some greenhouse gases, however, depending on the fuel used. Before this alternative can be adopted on a large scale, developers will need to ensure that it will offset substantially more greenhouse gas emissions than it would emit.

Sometime in the future, superconductor technology might also help. Superconductors are materials that can conduct electric current with very little energy loss. Presently, much of the electricity from a power plant gets lost during transmission along utility wires.

For now, though, most superconductor materials are effective only at extremely cold temperatures. If scientists ever develop a practical superconductor for use at atmospheric temperatures, electric power generation needs could drop dramatically. Greenhouse gas emissions would go way down too.

Power Policy Alternatives

Talking about alternative energy is one thing, but getting industries and consumers to switch to alternatives with lower emissions is another. As with most public policy issues, governments can use different tools to attain an objective. Some policies rely on voluntary action, while other types of policies force people into acting a certain way. Policy approaches vary in their scope and acceptability to the business community and the public at large.

So far, U.S. government policies on energy usage and greenhouse gas emissions have involved relatively little coercion. A June 2002 report by the U.S. Environmental Protection Agency summarized various programs, including minimum efficiency standards for new residential appliances and the Energy Star program to promote energy efficiency for homes and offices. The government also created some programs to promote alternative energy technologies. Critics like Philip Clapp of the National Environmental Trust have complained that programs that are mostly voluntary produce minuscule reductions in greenhouse gas emissions.

Tax incentives are another low-coercion policy option. For example, the federal or state government could reward renewable energy investments by allowing companies to subtract all or part of the investment from their tax bill. The reward of the credit would bring down the bottom-line cost of the investment.

Since state and federal governments buy a lot of electric power, they could make it a policy to use power generated from renewable resources instead of generated power from fossil fuels. In some instances, states actually have gone further. In return for allowing electric power plants virtual monopolies, they have required a percentage of the plants' power generation to come from renewable sources. Texas is an example.

Reporting is another policy option. The 1992 Energy Policy Act created voluntary reporting of greenhouse gases. The Energy Information Administration's report for 2000 included such reported information from 222 corporations, associations, and individuals.

In July 2002, the secretaries of Energy, Commerce, and Agriculture and the administrator of the U.S. Environmental Protection Agency recommended an expanded reporting system. Among other things, it would provide a better tool for the government to gauge success in cutting greenhouse gas intensity, the level of emissions in relation to the country's overall economic productivity. "Our goal is to significantly improve our reporting system, reduce the projected growth in greenhouse gases over the long-term, and credit those who voluntarily make real reductions in greenhouse gas emissions," noted Secretary of Energy Spencer Abraham. The technical guidelines of the voluntary reporting program were revised in 2007 to increase the accuracy and reliability of emissions measurements.

Reporting does not impose any obligation to cut emissions. But, as the public would be able to get emissions statistics from reports filed with the government, so companies with high levels of emissions may find themselves forced to cut emissions just to avoid public disapproval.

In 2005 Congress passed an updated version of the Energy Policy Act. It addressed energy efficiency, renewable energy, fossil fuels, and research and development in the field, among other topics.

At the opposite end of the policy spectrum is direct regulation of greenhouse gas emissions. In 2003, for example, Senators Joseph Lieberman (Dem.–CT) and John McCain (Rep.–AZ) introduced a bill for a proposed Climate Stewardship Act. The bill called for electric utilities, industrial plants, large commercial facilities, and the transportation sector to scale back greenhouse gas emissions to 2000 levels by the year 2010. By 2016, regulated entities would have to cut emissions back to their 1990 levels. Entities would be free to trade emissions allowances in order to comply with the law.

Emissions limitation policies would impose costs on regulated entities. They would have to buy new equipment or technologies to cut greenhouse gases, scale back production, or buy emission credits from other companies.

Depending on the market for any product or service, a company might or might not be able to pass all its costs on to consumers and maintain the same level of production and profitability. There could well be a drop in overall economic productivity.

On the other hand, direct regulation of greenhouse gas

emissions could boost the demand for development of new technologies to meet the limits. If that happened, then productivity would not necessarily have any substantial drop.

A carbon tax is another relatively coercive policy choice. In the simplest terms, governments would tax industries based on their calculated emissions of greenhouse gases. Instead of directly limiting emissions, a carbon tax would indirectly pressure companies to cut back on activities that produce high amounts of greenhouse gases. The tax would add to the company's final costs, which could reduce consumer demand for the product and could cause adverse impacts on the economy.

On the other hand, a carbon tax could benefit society. A report by Resources for the Future argues that a carbon tax on the electricity sector of $10 per metric ton could lead to health benefits worth $3 per metric ton from associated reductions in nitrous oxides and sulfur dioxide. Beyond that, the government could use the collected tax money to accomplish other socially worthwhile goals.

An energy tax is somewhat similar to a carbon tax. Instead of looking at end-of-the-line emissions, it would tax companies on their use of greenhouse gas intensive electricity sources. While it would be more indirect than a carbon tax, an energy tax might be easier to calculate and administer. Instead of offering voluntary incentives to switch to clean, renewable energy, an energy tax would punish companies that continued to produce high levels of greenhouse gases.

As a general rule of thumb, the more flexibility companies have in complying with emissions limits or other policies to reduce greenhouse gases, the less costly it will be for them to comply. Flexibility in timing, for example, can let a company take measures to meet new requirements when it is replacing or updating capital equipment. On the other hand, companies may not set a time for taking such actions unless they have market incentives or a legal deadline. In theory, a desire for flexibility could turn into an excuse to postpone action indefinitely.

To make matters more complicated, the benefits of policies to cut greenhouse gas emissions will not be immediately visible. Some effects of climate change take decades or even centuries to occur. The long-range nature of global climate change makes it hard for policymakers and many citizens to see how potentially costly measures today will make life better for future generations.

Obviously, this is a very simplified overview of some of the policy approaches the government can take to affect the mix of energy production and usage in the United States. Each approach is likely to draw opposition from companies and groups that stand to lose enormously if the measure is adopted. Each approach will involve some costs for different sectors of the economy.

On the Road Again

Transportation is another major contributor to the United States' greenhouse gas emissions. For decades, the government and environmental groups have asked people to cut back their use of fossil fuels. Such steps save money, may help slow global warming, and promote health.

But people do not want to feel deprived. Even in the face of rising prices and environmental problems, Americans want a high standard of living. Often, an attitude prevails that bigger is better.

Since the 1970s, environmental groups have told consumers that smaller, more fuel-efficient cars get more miles to the gallon. By using less gas, the cars pollute less. They save consumers money too. Yet throughout the 1990s, American carmakers sold many minivans, sport utility vehicles, and lightweight trucks. Americans said they wanted a clean environment, but they also wanted the roominess and convenience of huge cars.

Higher gasoline taxes could, in theory, end Americans' love affair with gas-guzzling cars. But, in reality, when gas prices rose during the summer of 2001, and again in 2007, consumers complained but continued to buy gas-guzzlers. Meanwhile, gasoline prices in the United States are still substantially lower than in Europe and various other parts of the world.

Higher gas prices would not necessarily affect everyone equally. Rich people would probably continue to drive huge cars as much as they currently do, while people with less money might not be able to afford the higher prices. In many parts of the United States, people feel that a car is a necessity. They need their cars to get to work, since most areas do not have good public transportation. These people would have less money left over for food, housing, and other needs.

Improved fuel efficiency could cut greenhouse gas emissions considerably. In 1993, the federal government joined with America's three largest automakers, Daimler-Chrysler, Ford Motor Company, and General Motors Corporation, to form the Partnership for a New Generation of Vehicles (PNGV). PNGV's goal was basically to reinvent the family automobile. New energy-efficient technologies would reduce emissions of both greenhouse gases and toxic air pollutants, help families save money, and reduce reliance on foreign oil. In theory, these energy-efficient vehicles would also help make U.S.-made vehicles competitive with foreign-made vehicles. In 2002, the Bush administration renamed the PNGV project the FreedomCAR program.

The three major automakers have each developed "concept cars" under the program. Most use lighter-weight materials, such as plastic, for body construction. The concept cars also use alternatives to the traditional gasoline-powered internal combustion engine.

ARE ELECTRIC CARS OUR ROAD TO THE FUTURE? A NUMBER OF DOMESTIC
AND FOREIGN AUTOMAKERS HAVE ALREADY STARTED DESIGNING—AND
IN SOME CASES, SELLING—CARS THAT RUN ON A COMBINATION OF GAS
AND ELECTRICITY.

Hybrid electric vehicles combine an electric motor with a small gasoline or diesel engine. The electric engine generates and stores electricity as the driver applies the brakes or cruises. The power is then available for fuel-intensive functions like acceleration and stop-and-go city traffic. The combination format gets rid of the need to "plug in" or recharge batteries, as was the case with early all-electric cars. Hybrid concept cars built by the Ford Motor Company, General Motors, and DaimlerChrysler get over 70 miles per gallon. Honda's Civic Hybrid and Toyota's Prius, already on the market, each get over 50 miles per gallon.

Fuel cells are another environmentally friendly option. Basically, fuel cells combine hydrogen with oxygen from the atmosphere. The reaction produces energy that drives the car. Instead of spewing out gases, the tailpipe would drip water.

Blending gasoline with other fuels could also cut down on emissions. Ethanol made from crop wastes is one possibility. "Ethanol is theoretically 100 percent renewable, unlike all other automotive fuels available today," notes engineering professor Roydon Fraser at the University of Waterloo. There would still be some greenhouse gas emissions, but levels might be lower than those for present fuels.

Newer technologies could do a lot to lower emissions. The price of the most efficient larger cars is still relatively high, although owners could save about $2,200 during the vehicle's life. Despite that, many customers continue to buy large, sporty vehicles that get less than 30 miles to a gallon (48 km to a l) of gasoline.

Like their counterparts in Europe, Americans may also need to rely more on public transportation. That requires individual commitment to change. It also calls for community planning and tax dollars to plan, build, and maintain good public transportation that serves twenty-first-century Americans wherever they live.

Making Lower Emissions the Law

New technologies will eventually make cars more fuel-efficient and less polluting, but some people do not want to wait. They want to accelerate the pace of fuel-efficient technology to force car companies to sell environmentally friendly cars.

Under a 2002 law, California will limit greenhouse gases from new cars and light trucks sold in the state. In 2004 and 2005, the California Air Resources Board set standards to curb emissions that included restrictions on idling vehicles and on diesel fuel. Automobile manufacturers will also have to adhere to regulations adopted in 2005 that require declining fleet average emissions for vehicles certified for sale, beginning with 2009 models.

Environmental groups love the new law. "The law is proof that America doesn't have to take global warming lying down," said Ann Notthoff of the National Resources Defense Council. Ten states, including many in the Northeast, had adopted the California clean car standard as of early 2007, while several others were considering it. Also, eleven state attorneys general wrote to President George W. Bush urging the federal government to set national standards.

"It's going to be so much more cost-effective and efficient if we have a national framework and national support for our activities," says Susi Moser of the Union of Concerned Scientists. Time will tell whether nationwide limits become the law.

Adapting to Change

Treaties, taxes, technology, and permits can limit the release of greenhouse gas emissions into the air, but greenhouse gases remain in the atmosphere for years. Their effects on climate do not happen overnight; they can take decades to develop. Even with actions to limit emissions, global climate change is likely to continue for some time.

One way or another, then, humans will have to deal with some consequences of climate change. The more societies can plan for and adapt to those changes, the fewer adverse consequences will result from climate change. Such actions may make sense even for areas where significant uncertainties remain.

The effects of climate change on hurricane intensity are open to substantial debate. Yet even in today's climate, tropical cyclones cause substantial suffering and economic loss. Climatologist Kerry Emanuel at the Massachusetts Institute of Technology wants to see preventive action:

> **There is a great deal that can be done both in the developed world and in developing countries to mitigate the threat hurricanes pose in the present climate. I am a strong advocate of doing those things, which include better construction, not building in storm-prone coastal strips, and (especially in the third world) having better evacuation plans.**

Similar actions can help people who presently live in areas that are prone to flooding.

Infrastructure improvements would also be a tremendous help, especially for developing nations. Despite all the technological progress that ushered in the new millennium, about a billion of the world's people still lack adequate drinking water and 2.4 billion lack basic sanitation. Better systems to supply those services would alleviate substantial problems relating to floods and droughts. Likewise, better transportation systems would make it more practical for people to evacuate in case of catastrophe. A better infrastructure would also speed emergency response actions.

Developing nations also need to improve their public health services. The better an area's health care system is, the better its people can prevent or treat diseases—whether or not those ailments are related to global climate change.

Economic growth also can help stave off some of the problems predicted because of global climate change. The higher a country's standard of living, the more resources it will have to adapt to change. At the same time, economic growth promotes political stability. That would be a good thing, no matter what the thermometer says.

Ideally, countries would pursue sustainable economic development. Sustainable development is economic activity that can be conducted over a long period of time without destroying the natural resources on which it depends. An example is promoting ecotourism and bio-prospecting for medicine in a rain-forest area, instead of burning the area to create farms where poor soils will support crops for just a few years. People need to be able to feed, clothe, and care for their children. To the extent they can do that and also preserve the environment, everyone will be better off.

Of course, these measures and others will cost money. In one sense, people can view the spending as a way to even out the scales. Since industrialized nations may have placed developing nations at risk of greater harm from potential climate change, it may be fair to expect them to pay to reduce those risks.

Alternatively, people can view the projects as a way to promote political stability and economic growth. That can mean a larger global market for goods and services.

Yet another alternative is to view the measures as a sound humanitarian move. No matter how the debate about global climate change turns out, the fact is that people are suffering and need help now. On the other hand, limited money and resources exist to cope with so many needs. If people were more willing to share their wealth, they could have already done a lot to reduce the problems of poverty and disease.

Most people think that global climate change is under way. In the political arena, Democrats and Republicans disagree on questions such as how fast America should take action and whether actions should be mandatory or voluntary. As time passes, both the federal and state governments are likely to adopt more measures to cut greenhouse gas emissions.

When the government does adopt such policies, it will take decades or longer for people to see any appreciable benefits from them. Even then, other countries may have increased their own emissions. While the rate of growth in emissions will be measurably slower, assessing specific benefits from taxes, emissions limits, or other measures may be very difficult.

The United States and the rest of the world's countries hope that in the coming years their economies will grow and their people will prosper. Meanwhile, the world's climate will continue to change in response to both greenhouse gas emissions and the whole range of natural factors that influence weather. One way or another, people will need to adapt to global climate change.

Notes

Chapter 1

p. 7, par. 1, "Word for the Wise," August 24, 1999.
http://www.m-w.com/wftw/99aug/082499.htm (Accessed
January 12, 2003)

p. 7, par. 2, "Cleveland Sets a Heat Record," *Cleveland Plain
Dealer*, April 17, 2002, p. A1; "Weather: USA," *USA
Today*, April 17, 2002, p. 16A; Barbara Stewart, "More
Heat, More Use of Water and, as a Result, More Drought,"
The New York Times, April 18, 2002, p. B4.

p. 7, par. 3, "Weather: Events: Severe Weather," *USA Today*,
April 18, 2002, p. 12A.

pp. 7–8, "Weather: Monday's Temperature Almanac,"
Cleveland Plain Dealer, April 23, 2002, p. B10; Jeff
Nesmith, "Bush, Gore Disagree in Earth Day Speeches,"
Cleveland Plain Dealer, April 23, 2002, p. A1.

p. 8, par. 1, Debbie Howlett, "Weather Extremes Push Spring
Aside," *USA Today*, May 20, 2002, p. 3A; John Horton,
"Flaky Weather Sets Record for Late Snow," *Cleveland
Plain Dealer*, May 21, 2002, p. A1.

p. 8, par. 3, Pete Bowles, Robert Cuza, and Bryan Virasami,
"Heat Does Not Spring Eternal; Winter Weather Comes
Back Today," *Newsday*, January 30, 2002, p. A7 (Queens
ed.); Tom Vanden Brook, "U.S. Basks in One of the Warmest
Winters Ever," *USA Today*, February 26, 2002, p. 1A;

National Climatic Data Center, "Climate of 2003: January in Historical Perspective," February 13, 2003. http://www.ncdc.noaa.gov/oa/climate/research/2003/jan/global.html (Accessed March 9, 2003)

p. 8, par. 4, Neil Genzlinger, "Three Seasons Will Do Just Fine," *The New York Times*, April 7, 2002, p. NJ1(E).

p. 8, par. 5, Parris N. Glendenning, "Dark Cloud Looms Behind Sunny Winter," *USA Today*, March 1, 2002, p. 9A; Barbara Stewart, "More Heat, More Use of Water and, as a Result, More Drought," *The New York Times*, April 18, 2002, p. B4(E).

p. 9, par. 4, Paul Brown. *Global Warming: Can Civilization Survive?* London: Blandford, 1996, pp. 12–13.

pp. 9–10, par. 1, U.S. Environmental Protection Agency, "Global Warming: Climate," 2002. http://www.epa.gov/global warming/climate/index.html (Accessed June 3, 2002)

p. 10, par. 4, Patrick J Michaels. "The Decline and Fall of Global Warming," in Laura Jones, ed., *Global Warming: The Science and the Politics*. Vancouver, Canada: The Fraser Institute, 1997, p. 23.

p. 10, par. 4, George S. Philander. *Is the Temperature Rising? The Uncertain Science of Global Warming*. Princeton, NJ: Princeton University Press, 1998, pp. 35–36.

pp. 10–11, Svante Arrhenius, "On the Influence of Carbonic Acid in the Air upon the Temperature of the Ground," *The London, Edinburgh, and Dublin Philosophical Magazine and Journal of Science*, April, 1896, p. 237. http://hps.elte.hu/~zagoni/Arrh1.htm *and* http://hps.elte.hu/~zagoni/Arrh2.htm (Accessed August 25, 2002)

pp. 11–12, IPCC, "Summary for Policymakers: A Report of Working Group I of the Intergovernmental Panel on Climate Change,"2001, p. 7. http://www.ipcc.ch/ub/spm22-01.pdf (Accessed June 13, 2002)

pp. 11–12, Natural Resources Defense Council, "California Gov. Gray Davis Signs Landmark CO_2 Pollution Measure; New Law Uses Power of American Know-How to Tackle Global Warming," press release, July 22, 2002. http://www.nrdc.org/media/pressreleases/020722.asp (Accessed August 17, 2002)

p. 12, par. 2, Philander, pp. 35–36; F. Sherwood Rowland, Ph.D., University of California at Irvine, e-mail communication, June 12, 2002.

p. 12, par. 3, National Research Council, *Climate Change Science: An Analysis of Some Key Questions*. Washington, DC: National Academies Press, 2001, pp. 9–11; Brown, pp. 57–58.

p. 14, par. 2, *A Guide to the Climate Change Convention and Its Kyoto Protocol*, preliminary version: Bonn, 2002, p. 40.

p. 14, par. 3, Energy Information Administration, "International Energy Outlook 1998, April 1998. http://tonto.eia.doe/gov/FTPRoot/other/ieo98h.pdf (Accessed August 24, 2002)

pp. 14–15, BP, "Primary Energy Consumption," 2002. http://www.bp.com.downloads/1110/primary_energy.pdf (Accessed January 12, 2003)

p. 15, par. 1, World Bank, World Development Report 2000/2001, pp. 292–293. http://www.worldbank.org/poverty/wdrpoverty/report/tab10.pdf (Accessed August 24, 2002) Population statistics are from John W. Wright, ed., *The New York Times Almanac*, New York: Penguin Reference Books, 2001, pp. 545, 687.

p. 16, par. 1, United States Environmental Protection Agency, "Global Warming: Emissions," May 20, 2002. http://www.epa.gov/globalwarming/emissions/index.html (Accessed June 3, 2002)

p. 16, par. 3, IPCC Working Group 1, "Summary for Policymakers," p. 13.

Chapter 2

p. 22, par. 1, Robert Cess, Ph.D., State University of New York, telephone interview, November 17, 1995.

p. 26, par. 2, Sierra Club, "Global Warming—Overview," undated. http://www.sierraclub.org/globalwarming/dangerous experiment (Accessed January 10, 2003)

p. 26, par. 4, Intergovernmental Panel on Climate Change, Working Group 1, "Summary for Policymakers: A Report of Working Group I of the Intergovernmental Panel on Climate Change," 2001, pp. 2–3.

http://www.ipcc.ch/pub/spm22-01.pdf (Accessed June 13, 2002)

pp. 26–28, par. 1–2, Ibid., pp. 2–3, 7, 12.

pp. 28–29, Gerald Meehl, Ph.D., National Center for Atmospheric Research, telephone interview, June 19, 2002.

p. 30, par. 3, Ibid.

p. 31, par. 1, Philip Ball, "Shake-up for Climate Models," Nature Science Update, July 1, 2002. http://www.nature.com/nsu/020624/020624-11.html (Accessed July 30, 2002)

p. 31, par. 3, Meehl interview.

pp. 31–32, Intergovernmental Panel on Climate Change, Working Group II, "Summary for Policymakers—Climate Change 2001: Impacts, Adaptation, and Vulnerability," 2001, p. 4, n. 6. http://www.ipcc.ch/pub/wg2SPMfinal.pdf (Accessed June 13, 2002)

p. 32, par. 1–2, IPCC Working Group 1, "Summary for Policymakers," pp. 13–15.

p. 32, par. 2, National Research Council, Climate Change Science: An Analysis of Some Key Questions, Washington, DC: National Academies Press, 2001, p. 18.

p. 32, par. 4, Meehl interview.

pp. 32–33, par. 1, IPCC Working Group 1, "Summary for Policymakers," pp. 13-15.

p. 33–34, Gerald A. Meehl, et al., "An Introduction to Trends in Extreme Weather and Climate Events: Observations, Socioeconomic Impacts, Terrestrial Ecological Impacts, and Model Projections," *Bulletin of the American Meterological Society*, March 2000, p. 413.

p. 34, par. 2, par. 4, Ibid., Kerry Emanuel, Ph.D., e-mail communication, June 10, 2002. *See also* Kerry Emanuel, "Anthropogenic Effects on Tropical Cyclone Activity," undated. http://wind.mit.edu/~emanuel/anthro.html (Accessed June 9, 2002)

pp. 34–35, IPCC Working Group 1, "Summary for Policymakers," p. 16.

p. 35, par. 2, Meehl interview.

p. 36, par. 1, Juan Forero, "As Andean Glaciers Shrink, Water Worries Grow," *The New York Times*, November 24, 2002, sec. 1, p. 3.

p. 36, par. 2, pp. 36–37, Ibid., Greenpeace, "Greenpeace Documents Disappearing Glaciers," press release, August 7, 2002. http://www.greenpeace.org/international_en//press/release?press_id=21793&campaign_id= (Accessed August 15, 2002)

p. 37, par. 1, A. A. Arendt, et al., "Rapid Wastage of Alaska Glaciers and Their Contribution to Rising Sea Level," *Science*, July 19, 2002, p. 382; Mark Meier and Mark B. Dyurgerov, "How Alaska Affects the World," *Science*, July 19, 2002, p. 350.

p. 37, par. 2, Jack Williams, "A Warning of Warming? Scientists Ponder the Ramifications of an Antarctic Ice Shelf's Breakup," *USA Today*, April 15, 2002, p. 8D.

p. 37, par. 3, E. Mosley-Thompson, et al., "Late 20th Century Increase in South Pole Snow Accumulation," *Journal of Geophysical Research*, February 27, 1999, p. 3877–3886; Bales, R. C., et al., "Accumulation over the Greenland Ice Sheet from Historical and Recent Records," *Journal of Geophysical Research*, December 27, 2001, p. 33, 813.

p. 38, par. 1, Intergovernmental Panel on Climate Control, Climate Change 2001: Synthesis Report—Summary for Policymakers, 2001, p. 9. http://www.ipcc.ch/pub/SYRspm.pdf (Accessed June 13, 2002)

Chapter 3

p. 39, par. 2, David Bjerklie and Dick Thompson, "Wait Till Next Time: If a Little Heated Water in the Atlantic Can Create Floyd, What Storms Will Global Warming Bring?" *Time*, Sept. 27, 1999, p. 38.

pp. 39–40, North Carolina Redevelopment Center. "Floyd by the Numbers," undated. http://www.ncredevelopment.org/floydoverview.html (Accessed June 11, 2002); Disaster Center, "Hurricane Floyd Reports," undated. http://www.disaster center.com/hurricf9.htm (Accessed June 11, 2002)

p. 40, par. 1, CNN.com, "Hurricane Mitch Termed Central America's Disaster of the Century," November 6, 1998. http://www.cnn.com/WEATHER/9811/06/mitch.02 (Accessed July 19, 2002)

p. 41, par. 2, Greenpeace, "Climate Chaos Brings Misery, Hunger and Pollution to Millions," press release, August 15, 2002. http://www.greenpeace.org/international_en/news/

details?news_id=22243 (Accessed August 15, 2002)

p. 42, par. 1, Gale E. Christianson. *Greenhouse: The 200-Year Story of Global Warming*, New York: Penguin Books, 1999, p. 230.

p. 42, par. 2, Rochelle Sharpe, "Drought Police Hanging Water Violators Out to Dry," *USA Today*, August 12, 2002, p. 1A; Charles W. Petit, "The Great Drying," *U.S. News & World Report*, May 20, 2002, p. 54.

p. 42, par. 3, NASA Jet Propulsion Laboratory Image Advisory, "NASA Instrument Reveals Extent of Largest Colorado Fire," June 18, 2002; R. Gregory Nokes, "Two Oregon Wildfires Become One Giant Inferno," *(The Portland) Oregonian*, August 9, 2002, p. A12.

p. 43, par. 2, U.S. Department of State, "UNEP Study Predicts Drop in Crop Yields Due to Climate Change," November 8, 2001, with UNEP Press Release, "Climate Change: Billions Across the Tropics Face Hunger and Starvation As Big Drop in Crop Yields Forecast," November 8, 2001. http://usinfo.state.gov/topical/global/climate/01110801.htm (Accessed June 23, 2002)

p. 43, par. 3, Susi Moser, Ph.D., Union of Concerned Scientists, telephone interview, July 31, 2002.

p. 44, Robin A. Fanslow, "The Migrant Experience," Ameri can Folklife Center, Library of Congress, April 6, 1998. http://memory.loc.gov/ammem/afctshtml/tsme.html (Accessed July 20, 2002) *See also* PBS Online, "Timeline of the Dust Bowl," undated. http://www.pbs.org/wgbh/amex/dustbowl/timeline (Accessed July 20, 2002)

p. 46, par. 4, Johns Hopkins University, "Extreme Precipitation Linked to Waterborne Disease Outbreaks," press release, July 31, 1999; "Analysis of the Association between Extreme Precipitation and Waterborne Disease Outbreaks in the United States, 1948–1994," *American Journal of Public Health*, August 2001, p. 1194. http://www.jhsph.edu/Press_Room/Press_Releases/extreme_precip.html (Accessed November 23, 2002)

p. 47, par. 3, Jonathan Patz, et al., "Global Climate Change and Emerging Infectious Diseases," *JAMA*, January 17, 1996, p. 217. *See also* "Global Climate Controversy," *JAMA*, August 7, 1996, p. 372 (criticisms of Patz article and rebuttal).

pp. 47–48, Elisabet Lindgren and Rolf Gustafson, "Tick-borne Encephalitis in Sweden and Climate Change," *The Lancet*, July 7, 2001, p. 16.

p. 48, par. 1, Centers for Disease Control and Prevention, "West Nile Virus: Questions and Answers," updated July 18, 2002. http://www.cdc.gov/ncidod/dvbid/westnile/q&a.htm (Accessed July 21, 2002)

p. 49, par. 1, Patz, et al., "Global Climate Change and Emerging Infectious Diseases," pp. 217–223.

p. 49, par. 3, United States Environmental Protection Agency, U.S. Climate Action Report 2002, p. 108.

pp. 49–50, Intergovernmental Panel on Climate Control, Climate Change 2001: Synthesis Report—Summary for Policymakers, 2001, p. 9. http://www.ipcc.ch/pub/SYRspm.pdf (Accessed June 13, 2002)

p. 50, par. 1, Moser interview.

p. 50, par. 2, Anthony J. McMichael, and Andrew Haines, "Global Climate Change: The Potential Effects on Health," *British Medical Journal*, September 27, 1997, p. 805.

p. 50, par. 3, Paul Brown. *Global Warming: Can Civilization Survive?* London: Blandford, 1996, pp. 95–97.

p. 50, par. 4, "Sea Level Rise Underestimated," *Chemistry & Industry*, March 4, 2002, p. 8.

p. 50, par. 5, Michael Powell, "Northeast Seen Getting Balmier," *Washington Post*, December 17, 2001, p. A3; Sierra Club Global Warming and Energy Program, "A Dangerous Experiment," November 2000, p. 2. http://www.sierraclub.org/globalwarming/dangerousexperiment/dangerous_experiment.pdf (Accessed January 10, 2003)

p. 51, par. 1, National Wildlife Federation, "State Birds Forced to Take Flight?" press release, March 5, 2002. http://www.nwf.org/climate/statemigratorybirds.html (Accessed July 21, 2002) *See generally* National Wildlife Federation and American Bird Conservancy, The Birdwatcher's Guide to Global Warming, 2002. http://www.nwf.org/climate/pdfs/birdwatchersguide.pdf (Accessed July 21, 2002)

p. 51, par. 2, A. H. Fitter, and R. S. R. Fitter, "Rapid Changes in Flowering Time in British Plants," *Science*, May 31, 2002, p. 1689.

p. 51, par. 3, John Whitfield, "Global Warming Wrecks Moths'

Rhythm," Nature Science Update, February 7, 2001. http://www.nature.com/nsu/010208/010208-8.html (Accessed July 23, 2002)

pp. 51-52, par. 1, T. Edward Nickens, "North America's Fish Feel the Heat," *National Wildlife*, June/July 2002, p. 42.

p. 52, par. 3, Ove Hoegh-Guldberg, Climate Change, Coral Bleaching, and the Future of the World's Coral Reefs (Greenpeace, 1999). http://www.greenpeaceusa.org/media/publications/coral_bleaching.htm (Accessed July 22, 2002)

p. 52, pars. 3 and 4, Greenpeace USA, "World's Coral Reefs Will Be Devastated Within 30 Years if Global Warming Is Not Checked," press release, July 6, 1999. http://www.greenpeaceusa.org/media/press_releases/99_7_6.htm (Accessed July 22, 2002)

pp. 52–53, Ove. Hoegh-Guldberg, et al., "Pacific in Peril: Biological, Economic and Social Impacts of Climate Change on Pacific Coral Reefs" (Greenpeace, October 2000), pp. 53–55. http://archive.greenpeace.org/~climate/science/reports/GR249-CoralBleaching3.pdf (Accessed August 15, 2002)

p. 53, par. 2, Moser interview.

p. 53, par. 4, Moser interview.

p. 53, par. 5, Sierra Club Global Warming and Energy Program, "A Dangerous Experiment," November 2000, p. 2. http://www.sierraclub.org/globalwarming/dangerous-experiment/dangerous_experiment.pdf (Accessed May 16, 2002)

pp. 53–54, Michael Powell, "Northeast Seen Getting Balmier," *Washington Post*, December 17, 2001, p. A3.

p. 54, par. 1, Tom Clarke, "Thaw Weakens Link in Antarctic Food Chain," Nature Science Update, February 27, 2001. http://www.nature.com/nsu/nsu_pd/010301/010301-8.html (Accessed April 17, 2002)

p. 54, par 2, Timothy Egan, "On Hot Trail of Tiny Killer in Alaska," *The New York Times*, June 25, 2002, p. F1.

p. 54, par. 3, *See* e.g., Julie R. Etterson and Ruth G. Shaw, "Constraint to Adaptive Evolution in Response to Global Warming," *Science*, October 5, 2001, p. 151.

p. 55, par. 1, Moser interview.

pp. 55–56, par. 1, Tom Wilson and Lou Pitelka, "Potential Ecological and Economic Impacts of Climate Change," *EPRI Journal*, March/April 1997, pp. 36, 38.

p. 56, par. 1, Edward Goldsmith, and Caspar Henderson, "The Economic Costs of Climate Change," *The Ecologist*, March-April 1999, p. 98.

p. 56, par. 5, William Cline. *The Economics of Global Warming*. Washington, DC: Institute for International Economics, 1992, pp. 309–311, 336.

p. 57, par. 2, Albert Gore, Remarks by the vice president at George Washington University, March 17, 1995. http://www.ibiblio.org/pub/archives/whitehouse-papers/1995/Mar/1995-03-17-vp-gore-on-climate-change.text (Accessed July 9, 2002)

Chapter 4

pp. 58–59, Sallie Baliunas, Ph.D., statement before the Senate Foreign Relations Committee, Subcommittee on International Economic Policy, Export and Trade Promotion, October 9,1997.

p. 59, par. 1–2, Ibid. *See also* Drew T. Shindell, et al., "Solar Forcing of Regional Climate Change during the Maunder Minimum," *Science*, December 7, 2001, p. 2149.

p. 59, par. 3, John L. Daly, "Days of Sunshine," undated. http://www.vision.net.au/~daly/solar.htm (Accessed March 5, 2003). *See also* John L. Daly, "Still Waiting for Greenhouse," 2003. http://www.vision.net.au/~daly/index.htm (Accessed March 5, 2003)

p. 59, par. 3, Judith Lean and David Rind, "The Sun and Climate," *Consequences*, winter 1996. http://gcrio.ciesin.org/CONSEQUENCES/winter96/sunclimate.html (Accessed July 9, 2002)

p. 59, par. 3, E. N. Parker, "Sunny Side of Global Warming," *Nature*, June 3, 1999, p. 416.

p. 60, par. 1, Richard S. Lindzen, Ph.D., statement to Senate Committee on Environment and Public Works, July 10, 1997.

p. 60, par. 2, Arthur B. Robinson, et al., "Environmental Effects of Increased Atmospheric Carbon Dioxide," Oregon Institute of Science and Medicine, 1998. http://www.oism.org/pproject/review.pdf (Accessed November 24, 2002)

p. 60, par. 3, Ibid.; Patrick J. Michaels. "The Decline and Fall of Global Warming," in Laura Jones, ed. *Global Warming: The Science and the Politics*. Vancouver, Canada: The Fraser Institute, 1997, p. 24.

p. 60, par. 4, Jeffrey Kiehl, Ph.D., National Center for Atmospheric Research, telephone interview, November 16, 1995. *See also* Kathiann M. Kowalski, "Taking the Earth's Temperature," *Odyssey*, April 1996, p. 3.

p. 60, par. 5, Michaels. "The Decline and Fall of Global Warming," pp. 28–33.

p. 61, par. 1, S. Fred Singer. "*Hot Talk, Cold Science: Global Warming's Unfinished Debate*," Oakland, CA: The Independent Institute, 1997, pp. 36–37, 42–55; S. Fred Singer, "Global Warming: Science Fact or Fiction?" The Independent Institute, February 15, 2000 [http://www.independent.org/tii/forums/000215ipfTrans.html (Accessed July 10, 2002)

p. 61, par. 2, Bjørn Lomborg. *The Skeptical Environmentalist: Measuring the Real State of the World*. Cambridge, UK: Cambridge University Press, 2001, pp. 279–280.

p. 61, par. 3, Fred J. Wentz, and Matthias Schabel. "Effects of Orbital Decay on Satellite-derived Lower-tropospheric Temperature Trends," *Nature*, August 13, 1998, p. 661; Roy Spencer, "Measuring the Temperature of Earth From Space," NASA Space Science News, August 14, 1998. http://science.nasa.gov/newhome/headlines/notebook/essd13aug98_1.htm (Accessed November 25, 2002)

pp. 61–62, par. 2, Eileen Claussen, "Climate Change: Myths and Realities," July 17, 2002. http://www.pewclimate.org/media/transcript_swiss-re.cfm (Accessed November 26, 2002)

p. 62, par. 1–2, Patrick J. Michaels, and Robert C. Balling, Jr. *The Satanic Gases: Clearing the Air About Global Warming*. Washington, DC: Cato Institute, 2000, pp. 155–157, 161–168.

p. 63, Laurie Goering. "Philippine Volcano Blamed for Flood—Scientist Had Predicted 'A Lot of Moisture' for Midwest after '91 Pinatubo Eruption," *The Seattle Times*, August 8, 1993, p. A1; Ian Olgeirson, "Global Temperature Is Lowest in Decade Due to '91 Volcano—'Shading' Caused by Pinatubo Slices Summer Readings in Both North and South," *Wall Street Journal*, March 8, 1993, p. B6(E); "Pinatubo's Eruption Led to Global Cooling, U.S. Scientists Report," *San Diego Union-Tribune*, July 7, 1992, p. A13; William K. Stevens, "Ill Winds Bring Both Flooding and Heat Wave; El Nino and Volcano Getting Some Blame for Extreme Weather," *Seattle Post-Intelligencer*, July 9, 1993, p. A3.

pp. 62–64, Lomborg, pp. 289–291.

p. 64, par. 2, Roger Pocklington. "Oceanography and Inferences from Time Series." in Laura Jones, ed. *Global Warming: The Science and the Politics*. Vancouver, Canada: The Fraser Institute, 1997, pp. 37–49.

p. 64, par. 5, Keith E. Idso, Ph.D., prepared testimony before the House Committee on Government Reform, Subcommittee on National Economic Growth, Natural Resources, and Regulatory Affairs, and House Committee on Science, Subcommittee on Energy and the Environment, October 6, 1999.

p. 66, par. 2, Robert Mendelsohn, and James E. Neumann, eds. *The Impact of Climate Change on the United States Economy*. Cambridge and New York: Cambridge University Press, 1999, pp. 315–330.

p. 66, par. 3, Richard M. Adams, et al., "A Review of Impacts to U.S. Agricultural Resources," Pew Center on Global Climate Change, February 1999. http://www.pewclimate.org/projects/env_agriculture.cfm (Accessed November 11, 2002)

p. 67, par. 1, Michaels, and Balling. *The Satanic Gases*, pp. 139, 171–176.

p. 67, par. 3, Paul Reiter. "From Shakespeare to Defoe: Malaria in England in the Little Ice Age," *Emerging Infectious Diseases*, January-February 2000, p.1.

p. 68, par. 1, Oxford University, "Global Warming Is Not Responsible for Malaria Increase in East African Highlands," press release, February 21, 2002 (quoting Hay) http://www.admin.ox.ac.uk/po/020221.shtml (Accessed November 22, 2002); Simon I. Hay, et al. "Climate Change and the Resurgence of Malaria in the East African Highlands," *Nature*, February 21, 2002, p. 905.

p. 68, par. 1, John Whitfield, "Link Between Climate and Malaria Broken," Nature Science Update, February 21, 2002 (noting the Hay study and Patz's criticism). http://www.nature.com/nsu/020218/020218-12.html (Accessed November 22, 2002)

p. 68, par. 3, Charli E. Coon, "Why President Bush Is Right to Abandon the Kyoto Protocol," Heritage Foundation, May 11, 2001. http://www.heritage.org/Research/Energy and Environment/BG1437.cfm (Accessed January 10, 2003)

pp. 68-69, Jonathan H. Adler. "Hot Air: Global Warming Is

Not a Threat to Health or the Economy; Plans to Address It Are." *National Review*, August 17, 1998, p. 36.

p. 69, par. 2, Thomas Gale Moore. *Climate of Fear: Why We Shouldn't Worry About Global Warming*. Washington, DC: Cato Institute, 1998, pp. 156–157.

p. 69, par. 3, Marlo Lewis, "The Anti-Power Act," National Review Online, Guest Comment, June 26, 2002. http://www.nationalreview.com/comment/comment lewis062602.asp (Accessed August 25, 2002)

Chapter 5

p. 73, par. 1, "United Nations Framework Convention on Climate Change" (UNFCCC), Preamble, 1992.

p. 73, par. 2, Climate Change Secretariat, "United Nations Framework Convention on Climate Change: Status of Ratification," February 17, 2003. http://unfccc.int/ resource/conv/ratlist.pdf (Accessed March 5, 2003) *See also* Climate Change Secretariat, "A Guide to the Climate Change Convention and Its Kyoto Protocol," preliminary version, 2002, p. 6. http://unfccc.int/resource/ guideconvkp-p.pdf (Accessed March 5, 2003)

p. 74, par. 1, UNFCCC, Article 3, Section 3; par. 2, UNFCCC, Article 3, Section 1; par. 3, UNFCCC, Article 4, Section 2.

pp. 74–75, F. Sherwood Rowland, Ph.D., University of California, Irvine, e-mail communication, June 12, 2002.

p. 75, par. 1, David G. Victor. *The Collapse of the Kyoto Protocol and the Struggle to Slow Global Warming*. Princeton, NJ: Princeton University Press, 2001, p. 33.

pp. 75–76, par. 2, Bill Clinton, "Remarks to the United Nations Special Session on Environment and Development in New York City," June 26, 1997, in Weekly Compilation of Presidential Documents, June 30, 1997, p. 973.

p. 76, par. 2, S.R. 98, 143 Congressional Record S8119 (July 25, 1997).

p. 77, par. 1, Gale E. Christianson. *Greenhouse: The 200-Year Story of Global Warming*. New York: Penguin Books, 1999, pp. 255–256; William K. Stevens, "In Kyoto the Subject Is Climate; The Forecast Is for Storms," New York Times Online, November 27, 1997. http://www.nytimes.com/ library/national/120197intro.html (Accessed May 21, 2002)

p. 77, par. 2, Michael Toman, ed. *Climate Change Economics and Policy*. Washington, DC: RFF Press, 2001, pp. 19–21.

p. 79, par. 3, Kyoto Protocol, Article 25.

p. 80, par. 1, George W. Bush, "Text of a Letter from the President to Senators Hagel, Helms, Craig, and Roberts," March 13, 2001. http://www.whitehouse.gov/news/releases/2001/03/20010314.html (Accessed August 13, 2002) *See also* "Mr. Bush Reverses Course," *The New York Times*, March 15, 2001, p. A24.

pp. 80–81, George W. Bush, "Remarks Announcing the Clear Skies and Global Climate Change Initiatives in Silver Spring, Maryland," February 14, 2002, in Weekly Compilation of Presidential Documents, February 18, 2002, p. 232.

pp. 81–82, par. 2, Thomas C. Schelling, "What Makes Greenhouse Sense? Time to Rethink the Kyoto Protocol," *Foreign Affairs*, May/June 2002, p. 2.

p. 82, par. 1, United States Environmental Protection Agency, "U.S. Climate Action Report—2002: Third National Communication of the United States of America Under the United Nations Framework Convention on Climate Change, 2002." http://www.epa.gov/globalwarming/publications/car (Accessed June 3, 2002)

p. 82, par. 1, "Remarks by the President to the Travel Pool," June 4, 2002. http://www.whitehouse.gov/news/releases/2002/06/20020604-16.html (Accessed June 5, 2002)

p. 82, par. 4, Susi Moser, Ph.D., Union of Concerned Scientists, telephone interview, July 31, 2002.

p. 83, par. 1, Kyoto Protocol, Article 25.

p. 83, par. 2, Al Gore, "The Selling of an Energy Policy," *The New York Times*, April 21, 2002, sec. 4, p. 13.

p 83, par. 3, Greenpeace, "Bush Caves In to Fossil Fuel Industry," press release, March 14, 2001 http://archive.greenpeace.org/pressreleases/climate/2001mar14.html (Accessed August 14, 2002); Sierra Club, "Bush Breaks Campaign Pledge, Risks Children's Future with Global Warming U-Turn," press release, March 13, 2001. http://lists.sierraclub.org/SCRIPTS/WA.EXE?A2=ind0103&L=ce-scnews releases&D=1&T=0&H=1&O=D&F=&S=&P=766 (Accessed August 14, 2002)

p. 83, par. 3–4, "Kyoto Protocol: Status of Ratification," January 12, 2003. http://unfccc.int/resource/kpstats.pdf (Accessed January 12, 2003) *See also* DW-World.DE, "Canada Signs Kyoto-Russia Next?" December 17, 2002.

http://www.dw world.de/english/0,3367,1429_W_715831,00.html
(Accessed December 18, 2002)

p. 84, par. 5, Moser interview.

pp. 84–85, Christie Whitman, "Memorandum for the President,"
March 6, 2001, reprinted in The Washington Post Online,
March 26, 2001. http://www.washingtonpost.com/
wp-rv/onpolitics/transcripts/whitmanmemo032601.htm
(Accessed May 16, 2002)

p. 85, par. 1, George W. Bush, "Remarks Announcing the
Clear Skies and Global Climate Change Initiatives in Silver
Spring, Maryland."

p. 85, par. 4, Moser interview.

p. 86, par. 1, Ibid.

p. 87, par. 1, William Chandler, et al., "Climate Change
Mitigation in Developing Countries," Pew Center on Global
Climate Change, October 2002.
http://www.pewclimate.org/projects/dev_mitigation.pdf
(Accessed December 1, 2002)

p. 87, par. 3, United States Department of State, "Climate
Action Partnership Announced Between Australia and the
United States," press statement, February 27, 2002.
http://www.state.gov/r/pa/prs/ps/2002/8545.htm
(Accessed August 17, 2002); United States Department of
State, "The U.S.–Australia Climate Action Partnership
Moves Forward," press statement, July 9, 2002.
http://www.state.gov/r/pa/prs/ps/2002/11744.htm (Accessed
August 17, 2002)

p. 87, par. 4, United States Department of State, "U.S.–India
Joint Statement on Climate Change," May 6, 2002.
http://www.state.gov/g/oes/rls/prsrl/press/jan/9964.htm
(Accessed 8/17/02). *See also* United States Department of
State, "U.S.-Italy 'Joint Climate Change Research Meeting,'"
press statement, January 23, 2002.
http://www.state.gov/r/pa/prs/ps/2002/7412.htm
(accessed 8/17/02); and United States Department of State,
"Second Meeting of U.S.–Japan High-Level Consultations
on Climate Change," press statement, April 5, 2002.
http://www.state.gov/r/pa/prs/ps/2002/9193.htm
(Accessed 8/17/02)

p. 88, par. 2–3, Toman, p. 20.

p. 88, par. 4, Global Climate Coalition, "The Impacts of the

Kyoto Protocol," May 2000.
http://www.globalclimate.org/KyotoImpacts.pdf (Accessed
August 12, 2002) *See also* Toman, p. 42; Victor, pp. viii–ix.

pp. 88–89, World Wildlife Fund, "New Report Disproves Bush
Claims That Global Warming Treaty Would Hurt U.S.
Economy," press release, July 12, 2001. http://www.
commondreams.org/news2001/0712-06.htm (Accessed
January 12, 2003)

Chapter 6

p. 91, George W. Bush, "Remarks Announcing the Clear Skies
and Global Climate Change Initiatives in Silver Spring,
Maryland," February 14, 2002, in Weekly Compilation of
Presidential Documents, February 18, 2002, p. 232; U.S.
Climate Change Science Program, "Strategic Plan for the
Climate Change Science Program," draft, November 19,
2002.

p. 94, par. 5, Neela Banerjee, "Economic Interests Keep Drive
for Renewable Energy Stuck in Neutral," *The New York
Times*, August 20, 2002, p. F9.

pp. 94–95, Natural Resources Defense Council, "Global
Warming: In Depth-Reported 'Reductions,' Rising
Emissions," November 2001. http://www.nrdc.org/
globalWarming/reductions/execsum.asp (Accessed August
19, 2002); and National Environmental Trust, "Electrical
Power," undated, citing January 2000 data. http://
environet.policy.net/warming/costs/electric.vtml
(Accessed August 18, 2002)

p. 95, par. 1, Natural Resources Defense Council, "Untangling
the Accounting Gimmicks in White House Global Warming,
Pollution Plans," February 2002. http://www.nrdc.org/
globalWarming/agwcon.asp (Accessed August 19, 2002)

p. 97, par. 3, John Thornton, Ph.D., National Renewable
Energy Laboratory, telephone interview, April 4, 2000.

pp. 97–98, John Benner, Ph.D., National Renewable Energy
Laboratory, telephone interview, April 4, 2000.

p. 98, par. 2, Banerjee, p. F9.

p. 99, par. 2, National Renewable Energy Laboratory, "Innovative
Utility Takes to the Wind," press release, July 19, 2002; Banerjee,
p. F9; Margot Roosevelt, "The Winds of Change," *Time*, August

26, 2002, p. A40.

p. 99, par. 3, "A Tale of Two Towers," 2001.
http://www.nyc24.com/2001/issue01/story04/bldg.html
(Accessed November 20, 2002)

pp. 100–101, United States Environmental Protection Agency,
"U.S. Climate Action Report-2002: Third National Com-
munication of the United States of America Under the
United Nations Framework Convention on Climate Change,
2002," pp. 50–69. http://www.epa.gov/globalwarming/
publications/car/ch4.pdf. *See* "Statement of Philip Clapp,
President of the National Environmental Trust on the
President's Power Plant and Global Warming Proposals,"
press release, February 14, 2002; "Statement of Philip
Clapp, President of the National Environmental Trust on the
Bush Administration's Climate Action Report: Report
Admits Global Warming Real, Does Nothing To Solve
Problem," press release, June 3, 2002.

p. 101, par. 2, Barry G. Rabe, "Greenhouse and Statehouse:
The Evolving State Government Role in Climate Change,"
Pew Center on Global Climate Change, November 2002,
pp. 12–15.

pp 101–102, Department of Energy, "Department of Energy
Sends Greenhouse Gas Registry Recommendations to White
House," press release, July 8, 2002.

p. 102, par. 2, S. 139, 108th Congress, 1st Session, discussed by
Sen. Lieberman in Congressional Record-Senate, 149
Congressional Record S. 166-67 (January 9, 2003).

p. 103, par. 1, Dallas Burtraw, et al., "Ancillary Benefits of
Reduced Air Pollution in the U.S. from Moderate Green-
house Gas Mitigation Policies in the Electricity Sector,"
Resources for the Future, September 1999.

p. 107, par. 3, Roydon Fraser, Ph.D., e-mail communication,
April 18, 2001.

p. 107, par. 4, Natural Resources Defense Council, "National
Security & Oil: 'Dangerous Addiction' Report Outlines
Risks of Import Dependence, Offers Roadmap to Save 5
Million Barrels Per Day," press release, January 16, 2002.

p. 108, par. 2 "California Governor Signs Bill to Curb Vehicle
Emissions," *Wall Street Journal*, July 23, 2002, p. D5; John
Cushman, "California Lawmakers Vote to Lower Auto

Emissions," *The New York Times*, July 2, 2002, p. A14.

p. 108, par. 3, Natural Resources Defense Council, "California Gov. Gray Davis Signs Landmark CO_2 Pollution Measure; New Law Uses Power of American Know-How to Tackle Global Warming," press release, July 22, 2002; *see also* "New York Legislator Eyes California Bill on Auto Emissions," *Wall Street Journal*, July 16, 2002, p. D4; James Sterngold, "State Officials Ask Bush to Act on Global Warming," *The New York Times*, July 17, 2002, p. 12.

p. 108, par. 4, Susi Moser, Ph.D., Union of Concerned Scientists, telephone interview, July 31, 2002.

p. 109, par. 1, Kerry Emanuel, Ph.D., e-mail communication, June 10, 2002.

Further Information

For Further Reading

Arnold, Caroline. *El Niño: Stormy Weather for People and Wildlife.* New York: Clarion Books, 1998.

Fridell, Ron. *Global Warming.* New York: Franklin Watts, 2002.

Friedman, Katherine. *What If the Polar Ice Caps Melted?* New York: Children's Press, 2002.

Green, Kenneth Philip. *Global Warming: Understanding the Debate.* Berkeley Heights, NJ: Enslow Publishers, 2002.

Haley, James, ed. *Global Warming: Opposing Viewpoints.* 2nd ed. San Diego: Greenhaven Press, 2001.

Hawkes, Nigel. *Climate Crisis.* Brookfield, CT: Copper Beech Books, 2000.

Maslin, Mark. *Global Warming.* Stillwater, MN: Voyageur Press, 2002.

Pringle, Laurence. *Global Warming: The Threat of Earth's Changing Climate.* New York: Sea Star Books, 2001.

Scoones, Simon. *Climate Change: Our Impact on the Planet.* Austin, TX: Raintree Steck-Vaughn Publishers, 2002.

Stein, Paul. *Forecasting the Climate of the Future.* New York: Rosen Publishing Group, 2001.

———*Global Warming: A Threat to Our Future.* New York: Rosen Publishing Group, 2001.

Warren, Dorothy. *Climate Change: A Resource for Students and Teachers to Support Teaching About the Nature of Scientific Enquiry and the Strengths and Limitations of Scientific Evidence.* London: Royal Society of Chemistry, 2001.

Organizations (including Web Sites)

Greenpeace, Inc.
702 H Street, NW
Washington, DC 20001
800-326-0959
http://www.greenpeaceusa.org

The Heritage Foundation
214 Massachusetts Avenue, N.E.
Washington, DC 20002
202-546-4400
http://www.heritage.org

Intergovernmental Panel on Climate Change
http://www.ipcc.ch

National Center for Atmospheric Research
Boulder, Colorado
http://www.ncar.ucar.edu/ncar/index.html

Pew Center on Global Climate Change
2101 Wilson Boulevard, Suite 550
Arlington, VA 22201
703-516-4146
http://www.pewclimate.org

Sierra Club
85 Second Street, Second Floor
San Francisco, CA 94105-3441
415- 977-5500
http://www.sierraclub.org

Union of Concerned Scientists
2 Brattle Square
Cambridge, MA 02238
617-547-5552
http://www.ucsusa.org

United Nations Framework Convention on Climate Change
http://unfccc.int

US Global Change Research Program
400 Virginia Avenue, SW, Suite 750
Washington, DC 20024
202-488-8630
http://www.usgcrp.gov

World Wildlife Fund
1250 Twenty-Fourth Street, N.W.
Washington, DC 20037
202-293-4800
http://www.worldwildlife.org

Bibliography

A. A. Arendt, et al. "Rapid Wastage of Alaska Glaciers and Their Contribution to Rising Sea Level." *Science*, July 19, 2002, p. 382.

Balbus, John, and Mark Wilson. "Human Health & Global Climate Change: A Review of Potential Impacts in the United States." Arlington, VA: Pew Center for Global Climate Change, 2000. http://www.pewclimate.org/projects/human_health.pdf (Accessed November 11, 2002)

Berger, John J. *Beating the Heat: Why and How We Must Combat Global Warming.* Berkeley, CA: Berkeley Hills Books, 2000.

Brown, Paul. *Global Warming: Can Civilization Survive?* London: Blancyor, 1996.

Burroughs, William James. *Climate Change: A Multidisciplinary Approach*. Cambridge and New York: Cambridge University Press, 2001.

Burtraw, Dallas, et al. "Ancillary Benefits of Reduced Air Pollution in the U.S. from Moderate Greenhouse Gas Mitigation Policies in the Electricity Sector." Resources for the Future, September 1999. http://www.rff.org/CFDOCS/disc_papers/PDF_files/9951.pdf (Accessed November 26, 2002)]

Christianson, Gale E. *Greenhouse: The 200-Year Story of Global Warming*. New York: Penguin Books, 2000.

Epstein, Paul. "Climate and Health." *Science,* July 16, 1999, p. 347.

Godrej, Dinyar. *The No-Nonsense Guide to Climate Change*. Oxford: New Internationalist Publications, 2001.

Goulder, Lawrence H. "Mitigating the Adverse Impacts of CO_2 Abatement on Energy-Intensive Industries." Resources for the Future, March 2002. http://webdev.rff.org/rff/ExternalFiles/ACF65.pdf (Accessed November 26, 2002)

Jones, Laura, ed. *Global Warming: The Science and the Politics*. Vancouver, Canada: The Fraser Institute, 1997.

Kolstad, Charles D., and Michael Toman. "The Economics of Climate Policy." Resources for the Future, June 2001. http://www.rff.org/disc_papers/PDF_files/0040REV.pdf (Accessed November 26, 2002)

Lempert, Robert J., et al. "Capital Cycles and the Timing of Climate Change Policy." Pew Center on Global Climate Change, October 2002. http://www.pewclimate.org/ projects/capital_cycles.pdf (Accessed November 26, 2002)

Luterbacher, Urs, and Detlef F. Sprinz. *International Relations and Global Climate Change*. Cambridge, MA: MIT Press, 2001.

Meier, Mark, and Mark B. Dyurgerov. "How Alaska Affects the World." *Science*, July 19, 2002, p. 350.

Mendelsohnn, Robert, and James E. Neumann, eds. *The Impact of Climate Change on the United States Economy*. Cambridge and New York: Cambridge University Press, 1999.

National Research Council. *Climate Change Science: An Analysis of Some Key Questions*. Washington, DC: National Academies Press, 2001. http://www.nap.edu/html/climatechange (Accessed December 1, 2002)

National Research Council. *Under the Weather: Climate, Ecosystems and Infectious Disease*. Washington, DC: National Academies Press, 2001. http://www.nap.edu/books/0309072786/html (Accessed December 1, 2002)

Newell, Richard, and William Pizer. *Discounting the Benefits of Climate Change Mitigation: How Much Do Uncertain Rates Increase Variations?* Arlington, VA: Pew Center for Global Climate Change, 2001. http://www. pewclimate.org/projects/econ_discounting.pdf (Accessed November 11, 2002)

Petit, Charles W. "The Great Drying." *U.S. News & World Report*, May 20, 2002, p. 54.

Philander, S. George. *Is the Temperature Rising? The Uncertain Science of Global Warming*. Princeton, NJ: Princeton University Press, 1998.

Rabe, Barry G. "Greenhouse and Statehouse: The Evolving State Government Role in Climate Change." Pew Center on Global Climate Change, November 2002. http://www.pewclimate.org/projects/states_greenhouse.pdf (Accessed November 25, 2002)

Singer, S. Fred. *Hot Talk, Cold Science: Global Warming's Unfinished Debate*. Oakland, CA: The Independent Institute, 1997.

Toman, Michael A., ed. *Climate Change Economics and Policy*. Washington, DC: RFF Press, 2001.

Toman, Michael A. "Moving Ahead with Climate Policy." Resources for the Future, October 2000. http://www.rff.org/issue_briefs/PDF_files/ccbrf26_toman.pdf (Accessed November 26, 2002)

U.S. Climate Change Science Program. "Strategic Plan for the Climate Change Science Program." draft, November 19, 2002.

United States Environmental Protection Agency. "U.S. Climate Action Report—2002: Third National Communication of the United States of America Under the United Nations Framework Convention on Climate Change." Washington, DC: Government Printing Office, 2002. http://yosemite.epa.gov/oar/globalwarming.nsf/content *and* ResourceCenterPublicationsUSClimateActionReport.html (Accessed December 2, 2002)

Victor, David G. *The Collapse of the Kyoto Protocol and the Struggle to Slow Global Warming.* Princeton, NJ: Princeton University Press, 2001.

Wigley, Tom. "The Science of Climate Change." Arlington, VA: Pew Center on Global Climate Change, 1999. http://www.pewclimate.org/projects/env_science.pdf (Accessed November 11, 2002)

Williams, Jack. *The Weather Book: An Easy-to-Understand Guide to the USA's Weather.* 2d ed. New York: Vintage Books, 1997.

Index

Page numbers in **boldface** are illustrations.

About the Author

Kathiann M. Kowalski has written eleven books and over 150 articles and stories for young people. She received her bachelor's degree in political science from Hofstra University and her law degree from Harvard Law School, where she was an editor of the Harvard Law Review. In addition to her writing career, Kathi has spent fifteen years practicing law, with an emphasis on environmental issues and litigation. Ms. Kowalski's various books have won awards from The Society of School Librarians International, the American Society for the Prevention of Cruelty to Animals, and The Pennsylvania School Librarians Association (PSLA).